STITCH MAGIC

WITH JAN BEANEY AND JEAN LITTLEJOHN

STITCH MAGIC

IDEAS AND INTERPRETATION

WITH JAN BEANEY AND JEAN LITTLEJOHN

BATSFORD

Acknowledgements

We would like to thank all those students and fellow embroiderers with whom we have worked both in this country and overseas. These experiences have offered us opportunities for sharing knowledge, crystalising ideas and forming friendships.

Thank you also to our families who have offered us every encouragement while we have been absorbed in writing this book together.

Our particular thanks must go to our husbands, Steve and Philip; to Victoria Udall for typing the text; to Hannah Littlejohn and Tom Fitzgerald O'Connor for proofreading; to the editorial staff at Batsford for their interest and support; to Michael Wicks, our superb photographer and finally the terrific students at East Berkshire College who constantly surprise us with their innovative stitching and who generously allow us to feature their work.

First published 1998
Reprinted 1999
First published in paperback 2005

Text, designs and line illustrations
© Jan Beaney and Jean Littlejohn 1998, 2005
Photographs © B T Batsford 1998, 2005

Photography by Michael Wicks
(except for page 83 where the photographs are
by Peter Read)

Designed by DWN Ltd., London

ISBN 0 7134 8960 X

A CIP catalogue record for this book is available
from the British Library.

Printed in Singapore by Kyodo Printing Co. Ltd

for the publishers

B T Batsford
Chrysalis Books Group
The Chrysalis Building
Bramley Road
London W10 6SP

www.chrysalisbooks.co.uk

An imprint of **Chrysalis** Books Group plc

The embroidery on page 2, Passages of Time 1, was inspired by a rock surface. The piece uses bonded cellophanes, plastics and scrim on a polyester ground and is machined on soluble fabric. Straight and cross stitches embellish the surface. **Jan Beaney**

Contents

Foreword

It gives me great pleasure to write this foreword for a most stimulating book. It will be a valuable asset to those who embroider already and visually informative to those who hope to learn. *Stitch Magic* cannot fail to create interest in the same way as Jan's previous book, *Stitches: New Approaches*. This one is notable for its great variety of hand stitches and the ways in which they can be manipulated. While focusing on hand embroidery, there is also a section showing combinations of both hand and machine embroidery, giving effects quite different from hand or machine stitching used alone. The contrast of a finely machine-stitched, coloured background with coarser hand stitching superimposed can produce very many colour variations with endless surface textures. The book shows some of the ways in which a stitch appears to vary, by using creative interpretations, such as differences in scale, the use of fine or coarse threads, the effect of placing stitches close together or far apart or working stitches over stitches.

The concept of the book is lively throughout, with clear text and notes on points to remember. There are suggestions on the choice of a stitch for a certain shape and purpose, with coloured illustrations making it easy to distinguish different threads and layering of stitches. My own books on embroidery were written without the benefit of colour and the colour photographs of the embroidered pieces here are an inspiring explanation of the methods. Most of them show stitches actual size in the samples worked with blown up details illustrated where appropriate with an explanation of the reason for the change in scale.

Those with little or no knowledge of embroidery may be unaware of its possibilities, for example how rich and effective surfaces can be with adaptations of just one stitch. With several stitches and different thread colours combined with an imaginative approach, a fabric may be transformed from a drab surface to an enchanting, jewel-like one. This magical element within the book should inspire any non-stitchers to 'have a go'. Packed with information, the ideas range from simple to more complicated examples. The photographs show bold patterns, geometric and freely worked patterns with strongly contrasting colour, subtle tones and delicate tints, a tribute to all those contributing embroiderers.

I have known Jan Beaney and Jean Littlejohn for a considerable time and admire them enormously for their endless enthusiasm which they convey to their students when teaching. Jan and Jean work as a team, but each has different ideas and particular interests. I must congratulate them on a book which is a treasure trove of ideas for both the beginner and the advanced student. Significantly they have continued to produce their own work in spite of teaching and researching their respective books. Both of them use drawing from observation and this forms the basis of many of their designs. With experiments, sometimes accidental ones, they have discovered new ways of stitching as well as qualities of new materials. Jan and Jean understand the problems encountered by students because they have solved many of them in the course of their own stitching.

Embroidery is addictive and as you learn more and more, you will find that it becomes increasingly fascinating.

Constance Howard

Istron Series: Night Path, where couching, straight stitches and speckling in fine silk threads have been built up on a background of midnight blue velvet.
Jean Littlejohn

Introduction

In the past surface stitches were mainly worked in a predictable manner, often to accompany appliqué. Most books categorized them into restrictive sections dictating certain stitches for particular jobs. Except for the innovative work of a few textile artists such as Rebecca Crompton, Constance Howard, Kathleen White and Eirian Short, it was only during the 1960s and '70s that people realised that a conventional approach to stitch could be counterproductive for creative work. Some embroiderers, fascinated by textural surfaces, seemed willing to experiment.

In 1985 *Stitches: New Approaches* was written (see Further Reading, page 141). This book did not underestimate the need to continue using traditional stitches for certain projects but offered another approach to creating stitched surfaces, giving a wider scope for an embroiderer's imagination. Emphasis was placed on stretching the rules of stitch making, crossing conventional boundaries to create a 'stitch dictionary' of marks and textures which would be suitable for the surfaces envisaged. Many questions and new thoughts were presented and a more varied approach towards stitching evolved.

We have written other books including stitch sections where elements such as line, texture, movement and linking mechanisms within a background were considered. This book was planned around the need to focus on this approach and develop further explorations of stitch. It is intended to co-ordinate and extend all the previous thoughts and develop them into new areas. A range of stitches will be exploited to show wonderful patterns indicative of environment, culture or custom. They can be developed as an extension of the ground cloth where the design, background considerations, colour and texture will be wholly appropriate for the type of surface visualized. Emphasis will be put on further developments of particular stitches, thoughts on the choices of thread and whether the colour, tone and texture will merge, blend or integrate sympathetically and sensitively with the pattern or imagery required.

As this philosophy towards stitch continues to progress, both forwards and laterally, it is hoped that much will be gained to encourage your personal journey. Your experience, attitudes, design sources, and the exciting range of threads, textural materials and methods now available, continue to change, giving each one of us endless creative routes to travel along.

We are both continually challenged and excited by stitched surfaces, and share the same philosophy, although at times offering and emphasizing different aspects and approaches in order to widen the stitch experience. In this book we each have chosen elements to develop with a secondary input from the other to balance and demonstrate a varied point of view. *Although many stitched samples are reproduced actual size, several have been enlarged to enable the details to be seen more clearly.*

The fascination of stitch, both ancient and modern, is totally absorbing, frustrating, soothing, exciting and always challenging. It is overwhelming and joyous to achieve from time to time the right balance of design and appropriate stitch which 'sits' comfortably within its background, creating a unique and beautiful effect. We have tried to convey our enthusiasm in an imaginative but straightforward manner. We have concentrated on some aspects in depth, suggesting variations for others, as well as offering new thought processes.

This book is fundamentally a celebration of stitch rather than a stitch dictionary – the aim is to experiment with and interpret stitches and enjoy the richness that stitching can bring. These experiences should enable you to plan and make a range of inspirational surfaces to suit a number of projects. We hope most of all to inspire you so that you can allow yourself time for creative play, in order to extend your stitch vocabulary.

A detail from a Nigerian carnival costume. Chunky twists of cloth and yarn have been couched down with torn strips of fabric to form an exciting bold design.

Historical Perspective

Handling and stitching into a piece of cloth echoes the rhythms of centuries. The origins of stitch lie in the necessity of joining skins or strips of fabric together to form a cloth large enough to wear, furnish a home, or act as a sail for a ship.

Some effective stitching was worked using quite primitive needles formed from fish or animal bones before the first bronze needles were invented. The needle is one of the most fundamentally unchanged tools in history and looking back at past embroideries of amazing skill and vitality, worked with the most simple of equipment, is very humbling.

Through the centuries some cultures have concentrated on woven or dyed textiles, whilst others, such as in parts of India, have a strong history of stitched textiles. They offer stunning examples of how magnificent embroidery can be when the design, the materials and the stitches combine to form a satisfying whole.

Before the widespread growth of trade, stitchers used the materials in their immediate environment and the techniques, colours, fabrics and patterns formed the traditions for their culture. Trading gradually offered a wider range of materials and today there is an overwhelming choice at our disposal. Despite the incorporation of new materials, the traditions often shine through. By developing and changing we keep our stitch heritage alive.

There are those who lament the passing of what they perceive as sound traditional technique and feel that we should aspire to the sheer re-creation of past glories. However, what we now accept as a tradition was once an innovation created by adventurous people using their materials in an imaginative way. We can respect their skills and develop our own innovative approaches to fabric and thread, inspired by their example. We can gain so much by looking at old textiles, the secret being to tap into their excitement and energy without simply copying or appropriating their culture. By looking closely at stitches, colour combinations, patterns and symbols, we can refresh and enrich our own approach to stitching.

Inspired by the floral patterns from traditional Hungarian embroidery, this celebrates a rich stitch tradition. Produced on a silk strip woven ground with a range of hand stitches including chain, detached chain (lazy daisy), satin stitch, straight stitch and French knots. **Fiona Fletcher**

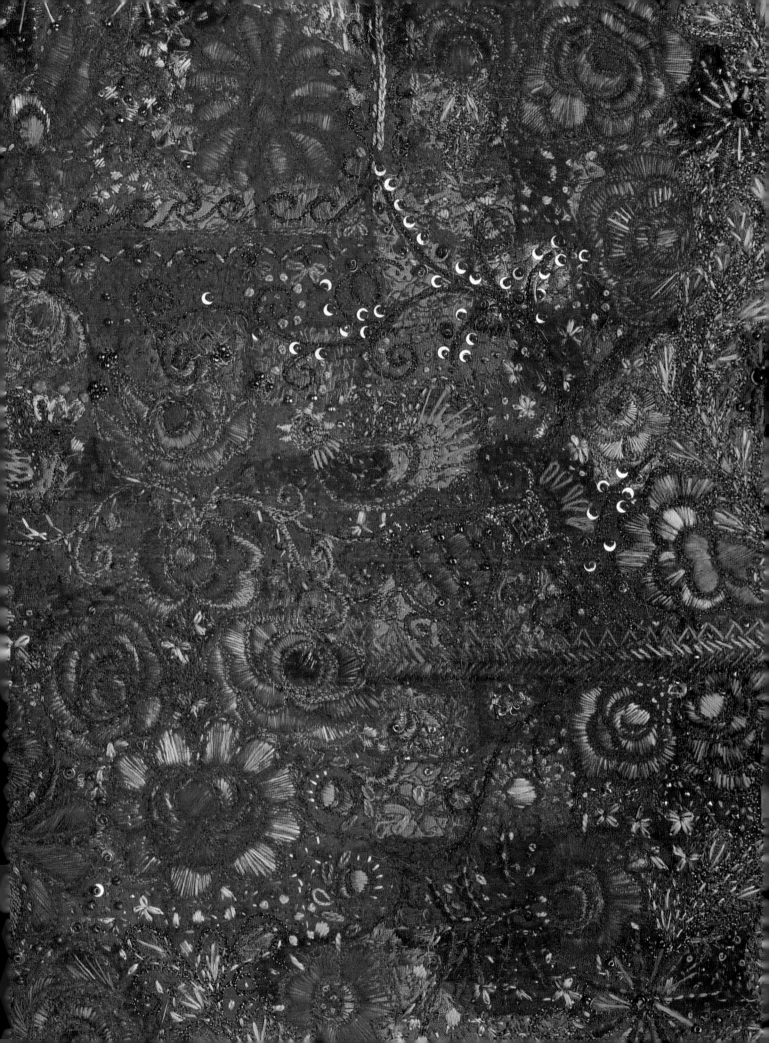

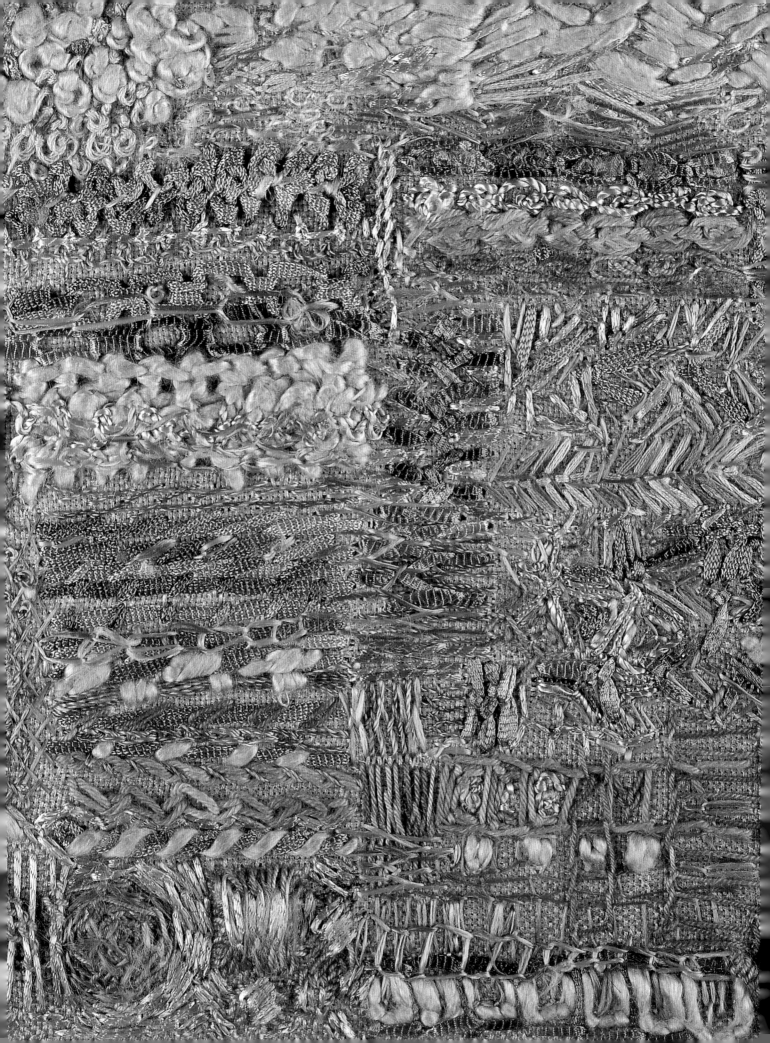

1

Beginnings

Whether you are experienced or new to stitching, it doesn't really matter. You can learn something fresh from picking up a piece of fabric, a few threads and a needle. These simple preparations will open the door to the richness of stitched surfaces.

Starting with Stitches

For the novice, just starting can be a daunting prospect. There are some strategies that will help you get going and will keep you focused. First, find a suitable decorative basket and use it to keep a simple range of threads, needles and scissors. If you use one, your frame should live there too, along with your background fabric. This will enable you to have everything you need to hand for those odd moments when you can fit in some stitching. In twenty minutes you can make a real difference. If however, everything is put away and takes effort to find, this is an initial disincentive.

Not everyone uses a frame, but having both hands free to stitch can be an advantage. When working quite long, straight stitches, a taut surface is easier – this is because the fabric can pucker on a loose fabric and therefore lose the crispness which makes it so effective. However, remember that the effect you are seeking should always structure your working method. Many people enjoy the movement of the cloth in the hand and the distortion can be a positive advantage. Embroiderers such as Julia Caprara who work in this way use the undulations and ripples created by the stitching to produce wonderfully atmospheric and rhythmic textiles which are enhanced by the quality of the surface (see pages 98–9).

The mere word 'samplers' conjures up a formal, disciplined stitched piece but you should remember that samplers were originally pieces of cloth on which people tried out new techniques. Imagine the excitement generated by groups of friends meeting to pass on newly found skills and stitches. So samplers will always have a part to play. For example, if you always use the same stitches, you can discover fresh textures and effects by experimenting on a sampler, and make it organized or spontaneous depending on your work method. An easy-to-stitch-into cloth is advisable for ease of working, but some of the experimental grounds described later (see pages 22–29) could be used successfully and innovatively in this way and give your sampler a contemporary feel. Keep notes with references to threads and fabrics for future ideas. Leave your sampler out on a notice board as a constant reminder and add to it as new ideas occur. Perhaps in four hundred years it will shed light on the ideas and work methods of today!

This detail of a sampler on a shaded linen ground contains textures and marks in a range of stitches. The straight stitch 'family' has been developed in different qualities of thread – including seeding stitch, running stitch, cross stitch and herringbone stitch. Chain variations have also been worked – such as zig zag, ladder or open chain, detached chain or lazy daisy, raised chain band and knotted cable chain. A range of couching effects, including French and bullion knots, are also featured. On a sampler of this nature, you can be totally free and arrange it just as you choose – because it acts as a stitch reference and a visual reminder when selecting stitches for a particular effect.
Jean Littlejohn

To concentrate effectively on the quality of the mark and texture of stitches, a simple strategy uses threads of limited colours exploiting cast shadows and rhythmic patterns. With more experience, you can then add other elements. A limited colour range also encourages an adventurous approach. From the very finest machine threads to thick torn fabrics, anything goes!

When working even the most humble stitched area, it is good practice to mark or stitch the boundary. It is then possible to develop sensitivity to composition within a shape rather than using unco-ordinated textures with no real framework. Composition needs careful thought because you can become so involved in the the variety of elements that you neglect the whole image. This is due to the intimacy of the technique and that you can become overly concerned with details. Always identifying the edge and relating the stitching to it sharpens up compositional skills. Reviewing the piece from a distance or holding the work up to a mirror will expose quite obvious difficulties, overlooked because of your familiarity with, or proximity to, the image.

When new to stitching it is often easier to fill the whole area than to leave awkward background spaces. With more experience in blending and integrating stitches (see pages 78–89), working positively with sensitive background shapes becomes easier.

Among many starting points, rubbings or printed surfaces which cover most of the area can give confidence. Alternatively create exotic stitches with a manufactured patterned fabric and cover it liberally in hand stitching using your own colour range.

Experiments with a single stitch and its infinite possibilities have promoted wonderful stitched surfaces and this should not be underestimated as a way of enriching your stitch vocabulary.

This richly stitched piece celebrates the texture of pure stitch. The inspiration for the sample was a transfer crayon rubbing from an Indian printing block. The task was to cover the whole ground with stitch in a monochromatic colour scheme. We can be easily seduced by the range of exotic effects which can be achieved, so the simple exercise of using threads in a limited colour range is always refreshing. Stitches used include detached chain, couching and French knots. **Amanda Martin**

Where Next?

Sometimes you need a fresh impetus to add some vitality and an unexpected element into your stitching. Surprising yourself is difficult and it is all too easy to fall back on what you are used to, like tossing a coin and then not acting on the result.

A strategy which has worked with classes of experienced and less knowledgeable stitchers alike is to have lists of stitches and characteristics. From this you accept a random selection and work with it, like it or not. Strangely enough, people tend to work more innovative samples when confronted with a selection they don't really relish. The 'Stitch Challenge' below gives a suggested palette.

Stitch Challenge 1

1 Buttonhole – regular – diagonal

2 Ladder chain – irregular – square

3 Cretan – regular – vertical

4 Fly stitch – irregular – triangular

5 Bokhara couching – regular – circular

6 Twisted chain – irregular – haphazard

7 Herringbone – regular – horizontal

8 Detached chain – irregular – meandering

This is a sample selection but, of course, there are many others which could be used. If you use the one listed here then select three random numbers from 1 to 8 to be absolutely unbiased and work with the result. Alternatively, you could ask a member of your family to select for you and make sure you don't cheat. This is a proven method of injecting freshness into your stitching. If, for example, you choose the numbers 1, 3 and 8 then you need to use regular Cretan stitch in a meandering rhythm.

Having worked the stitch in this way cross the first selection from the lists and make another selection. Using this approach you could work through the whole list and concentrate on interesting ways in which you can respond to the challenge. Some will be a great deal more difficult than others so it will really stretch your lateral thinking and development of using stitch innovatively. If this approach proves helpful then add different fabrics and threads and work on a larger scale.

The examples on the facing page show three interpretations of buttonhole stitch using the same threads and colours but different word combinations (see caption below). The regular element here is the size of the stitch.

*Three samples by **Jean Littlejohn***
(Above) Buttonhole – regular – square (1, 1, 2)
(Middle) Buttonhole – irregular – diagonal (1, 6, 1)
(Below) Buttonhole – regular – haphazard (1, 5, 6)

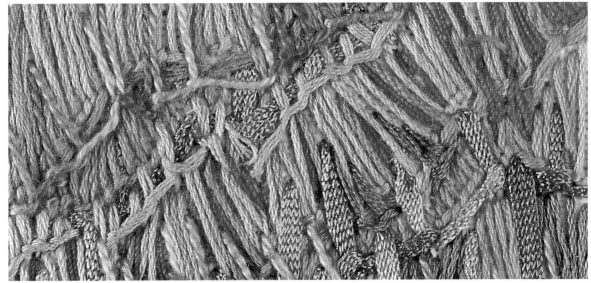

Stitch Challenge 2

1 Interlace

2 Tie or knot

3 Whip

4 Wrap

5 Add beads

6 Oversew

7 Needleweave

8 Distress

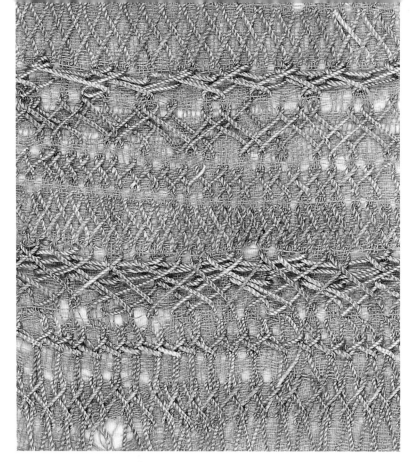

(Right) Herringbone – horizontal – irregular – distressed. **Diana Hammond**

(Below) Twisted chain – square – regular – whipped. **Yvette Swan**

Having established that the first challenge is a useful method of extending your stitch vocabulary, then further elements can be added. A fourth column with additional attributes will really stretch the problem solving involved and re-emphasize the extensive palette available to the embroiderer.

Now you can choose a new set of stitches and elements or continue to use the list in Stitch Challenge 1 by selecting four numbers. Choosing 1, 1, 2 and 5 will produce regular buttonhole worked in squares and with beads (see illustration below left).

There are very few stitches that cannot be developed in this way, and tackling some unpromising candidates could provide a new way of working. You can also use colours and printed and applied fabrics in order to achieve some of the characteristics. This is a real opportunity which you can use from time to time in order to ensure that you don't fall back on the familiar stitches that you can work with ease. It is not necessary to discard your favourites but the extra vitality that an injection of innovative stitching will provide may take you over a barrier into new exciting stitched surfaces. The added bonus is that if you do not wish to have them as samples they may be simply mounted and used as special cards or small panels.

*(Below) Sample by **Jean Littlejohn** (see main text).*

*(Below) A further development of this approach, but on a coloured ground and using a vegetable bag as a grid for blocks of twisted chain. **Jean Littlejohn***

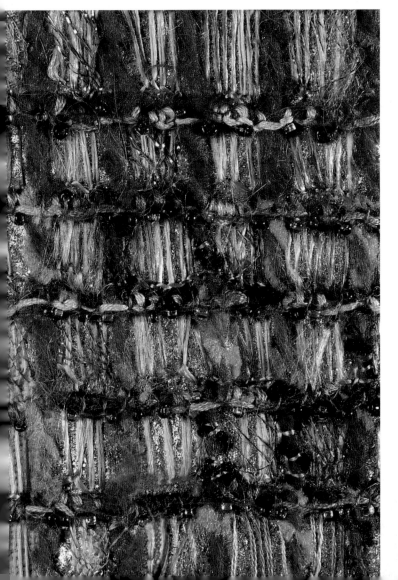

Planning to Stitch

Experimenting with stitches gives you increasing awareness of their properties and possibilities but eventually you need to exercise judgement over using them in your work. Before stitching there are some points which might help you avoid falling back on predictable techniques. Firstly, look at the imagery and note words which describe these characteristics. 'Organic', 'fluid', 'linear', 'fragmented', 'staccato', 'undulating', 'smooth' and 'rough' could be words which give clues for stitch. The texture and quality of the background combined with the appropriate stitches should reflect these key words.

The colours then need to be selected with careful regard to tonal values. The stitched mark can be quite dramatic and the wrong texture and tone make it inappropriate for the image.

Ask yourself what the stitching aims to achieve. Is it pattern, movement and blending, mark-making, texture or a combination of these? Chapter 6 highlights a range of alternatives, as suggestions to inspire you to develop your own approaches. When looking at the embroideries, bear in mind their stitch language and how they have achieved their effect. Analysing stitching which appeals to you allows you to sharpen your critical faculties and apply more sensitive judgment to your own work.

An 'inspiration board' is a useful device for gaining insight into your source material. It is useful to have something to pin into, such as polystyrene, cork board or insulation board, and these work really well at A2 or AI size. Collect a range of influences – cuttings, drawings, fragments, fabrics, threads and colour ideas. All these elements, as well as samples, combine to give a more complete picture than one image. Keep the board in an obvious place and add material as you come across it.

When working on a subject such as a Scottish landscape, using one image may encourage the interpretation of every piece of heather and you will become bogged down with detail. If however, you were to assemble a range of images, the epic proportions of the landscape would become more obvious and promote atmospheric imagery capturing the spirit of the subject rather than a slavish adherence to detail. Selecting aspects of your inspiration which appeal allows you to achieve a creative synthesis which gives the work integrity.

Through the water the stones seem like disjointed fragments fractured by light.

This inspiration board contains drawings, design ideas, fabric samples, threads, fabrics, wrapping paper and paper grids, assembling an image of an underwater mosaic. This process crystalised an initial uncertainty about how to work this idea. A Byzantine art programme was a further inspiration, so a television advertisement was added. Notebook references such as 'Through the water the stones seem like disjointed fragments fractured by light' help to work out atmospheric imagery. Having such a board on constant view helps to interpret ideas. **Jean Littlejohn**

2

Backgrounds

It is exciting to experiment with materials and combine them to form exotic samples, but when using them in finished work they should sit happily together to form a relevant background. There is an enormous bank of methods to use and you need to exercise restraint when selecting techniques for the image. Gimmicks will look superficial and date the work.

General Considerations

Keep a note of different effects in a notebook so that you have the details of the working processes in an accessible place. Will you really remember how you did that gorgeous background next year if you don't write it down? Bearing this in mind, there are various starting points which could prove useful.

Try to have an image or theme in mind when compiling materials to help the colour, rhythm and dynamics of the piece. With a rough, dramatic source of inspiration, for example, the quality of surface, the materials used and the application of colour and texture should reflect the subject and carry the idea forward (see Inspiration for Texture, page 115).

A palette knife is useful for building up dramatic layers of texture with a combination of materials. Similarly a calm and serene image will require a flowing and rhythmic application of stitch and colour to enhance the mood. Sponges when brushed on the surface in gentle sweeps, give a soft quality.

When working on functional items remember to consider that they will be used practically. Mixed media additions could prove difficult for washing and dry cleaning. Test any material or technique you are unsure of by washing or dry cleaning a sample. This is most important when selling work. In the future, galleries displaying textiles may well require to know the composition of

work for fire regulations and expect free-hanging textiles to be fire retardant.

When building up layers of bonding and textured surfaces, the resulting fabric can be quite stiff, making hand stitch more difficult, so test it first. It may also restrict the type of thread you use and leather or other heavy duty needles may be necessary.

Imagery and inspiration for the work could heavily influence the choice of materials. Various plastics and cellophanes, when used sympathetically, are employed to good effect. They shrink when heated and this could look superficial but they distort in an organic and logical way which is ideal for natural sources such as animal scales, tree bark, rocks and minerals. If, however, they are stuck on the surface without sensitive incorporation, they are valueless. Surface texture gels and expanding media are other useful additions if applied well to form part of a total image.

When using any of these materials, take care over health and safety and work in a well-ventilated space wearing a mask.

Piecing

When piecing backgrounds, select fabrics which promote the image or serve the required function. The use of pieced fabric grounds for stitched textiles is not widespread, which is a pity as the resulting cloth can offer an energy difficult to achieve on a

one-piece ground. See the Hungarian piece by Fiona Fletcher on pages 10–11, worked on a woven pieced silk ground.

There are numerous seams – run and fell seams, French seams, decorative open seams, to name a few – each with its own characteristic, which can be combined to good effect. The use of a stitch technique with historic resonances will draw the onlooker into a greater understanding of the integrity of the work.

They could also prove very useful in atmospheric memory pieces where they can reinforce the imagery.

Arctic Expressions series: To Please the Caribou, one of a series inspired by Arctic imagery, the life of a Caribou Inuit and the raw energy of the hunt. The background is a photo transfer from an acrylic painting on cotton with overlays of dyed Bondaweb and scrim. Stranded cotton and copper wire add vigorous marks to enhance movement. **Sandra Meech**

Bonding

Fusible web, Bondaweb and Wonder Under are all names of bonding materials. There are many brands on the market and they have subtly different properties. Most are sold with non-stick paper backing which can be very useful.

This sheer fabric glue has amazing possibilities for designing and creating backgrounds. Used conventionally, it is ironed on to the reverse of fabric, cut into the desired shape and, after the removal of the backing, applied sticky side down on to the ground fabric and ironed to secure. The quality of the surface may be subtly altered and stiffened, so bear this in mind when selecting sensitive and delicate fabrics. It also offers a slight resistance to hand stitching and for some people this might be unacceptable. Having said this, its versatility is limitless.

A big advantage of this method is that a wide range of fabrics may be used in this way. Although ironing on to a pale cloth gives a clear pattern and colour, darker fabrics may be used very successfully for dramatic backgrounds. Try ironing over patterned or dyed cloths for unexpected results. Some quite unpromising fabrics can be made usable in this way. Sheer fabrics are a good way of achieving an atmospheric effect when coloured using this method.

Bondaweb with Foil

There are a number of heat foils on the market – some of which are specifically designed for fashion fabrics – which prove useful for embroidered grounds. These are fine layers of metal supported by a transparent heat-resistant layer. They come in a wide range of colours and some patterns, many of which are quite garish. Like many other products for fashion fabrics, the embroiderer can make good use of them. Craft specialists stock these foils, but you can also experiment with those sold for use with computers (this is only appropriate for use for work which is decorative, rather than functional). The foils may be used on pale or dark colours and on a variety of surfaces. These surfaces are so seductive that they can be overused, so discretion is advised – otherwise you will end up swamped with 'glitzy' surfaces.

Heat transfer foils with bonded surfaces offer the possibility of jewel-like sensitive grounds. First iron off the Bondaweb or fusible web onto the background in the usual way and then remove the silicone backing (the Bondaweb may be coloured first, see below). Reduce the iron to its wool setting, as this will not work if it is too hot. Then place the heat transfer foil, with the coloured or shiny side uppermost, on to the bonded surface.

As a precaution, place baking parchment over the top before ironing. With a heavy hand a solid metallic surface will emerge, but with the gentlest of touches a mere shimmer is possible and the foil may be reused many times until all the metallic surface has been transferred. The more sparse the foil becomes the more sensitive the imagery and, in this way, iconic images and ancient distressed gilded surfaces can be achieved. Further colouring or appliqué can take place over the metallic surface.

Bondaweb with Colour

An exciting use of Bondaweb is the application of colour to the surface before ironing off. Liquid colour may be painted or sponged on the rougher (glue) side of the bonding material. Silk paints work well, as do acrylic paints, which can be mixed with water and used on fabric. The glue sheet wrinkles against the backing paper when wet, causing ripples and rivulets of pattern. When dry this can be ironed off on many fabrics, transferring the image on to a cloth. Iron on fabric using a hot setting and be careful to iron down the edges. Peel the paper back gently to reveal the pattern. If it does not peel easily, then iron for longer and allow to cool briefly before peeling back. The paper will stick if the colour is not dry. Brush the colour gently as rough handling could crack the bonding surface. A light sponge works well.

Should a particular rhythmic look be required, such as for sea water, it will be necessary to apply the colour in a particular direction so the ripples always work one way – always test first. This effect is difficult to achieve in any other way. Patterns created using this method may need further embellishment and because this is essentially a bonding material, further heat can reactivate its fusing properties. Fragments of thread or shredded fabric may be sprinkled into the coloured bonded surface and

after placing baking parchment over the top and ironing it, the textures will bond. Always be aware of the tone and quality of these additions to achieve a sensitive, integrated background.

Initially there is a slightly sticky feel to the surface which does eventually wear off. If you wish to achieve this effect and absorb the tacky surface then place a very fine, almost transparent, chiffon scarf over the top and, with baking parchment covering the cloth, bond it and seal the surface.

Brightly painted Bondaweb was ironed onto a black fabric and heat transfer foil was gently applied with the lightest of pressure by ironing on a wool setting. Having achieved a distressed effect various stitches, such as straight and couching, were worked. This interprets a happy day spent in New York looking at the buildings and an exhibition of Byzantine art at the Metropolitan Museum. **Jean Littlejohn**

Textured Surfaces

There is a bewildering array of products for creating textured surfaces. Time spent experimenting is always useful but it is advisable to have the surface quality in mind in order not to experiment just for the sake of it. These techniques are available to promote your ideas, not to dictate them.

You can use texture gels, liquid acrylic wax, dimensional paints, gesso, heat expanding media and numerous others with or without colour and iridescent paints which can be added to enrich them. These materials add another layer to a fabric and may be stitched into, or used on their own. *Dimensional paints* are supplied in small squeezy bottles or tubes and when used to apply shapes or textures to a surface and allowed to dry, the paint application retains its shape. Similarly texture gels will give a surface texture, or they will mix with the threads to add body to the stitching (see page 119). *Acrylic waxes* have a cloying quality which offers a waxier surface when working with a mixed media ground. Unlike melted wax they are used cool and stay fluid for much longer, making them useful for specific effects. Gesso has long been used for priming canvas. With fabric backgrounds it can be watered down to texture film which is excellent for distressed effects on the fabric. As always when building up backgrounds, materials need to be integrated into the composition in order not to look 'gimmicky'. Different ways of applying these materials will offer a range of effects. Paintbrushes, sponges, palette knives, stippling and printing all provide different surface qualities.

Burning and heat fusing with soldering or heat embossing tools will alter the surface of synthetic fabrics. Such fabrics frequently have a compelling shiny surface but by gently offering heat to the surface, bubbling and distortion may take place and render the fabric more sympathetic to stitching. Synthetics with piled surfaces, such as velvets, can be altered dramatically with soldering or pyrography irons. Layers may be built up and fused, creating sculptured cloths. Always be aware of fumes; remember to work in a well-ventilated area and wear a mask.

Similarly, plastics, cling film, bubble wrap and other materials which shrink and melt with heat may be used. Mixed with grated wax crayons, fibres and threads, fragile and lace-like textures emerge when placed between two layers of baking parchment and ironed. Too much wax will swamp the texture and too little will leave an insensitive harsh plastic surface, so experiment to find the most successful combination.

Tyvek which shrinks with heat has been popular but can look too obvious if not well incorporated. Manufactured in various thicknesses, it is designed for jobs where a tough, non-porous flexible fibre is needed. When exposed to heat it buckles and bubbles easily. Colour it in various ways both back and front, sandwich it between two layers of baking parchment and iron to gain full effect. More predictable effects may be achieved with the point of the iron. Lace-like holes can occur as part of the natural process but if on first ironing you lift the iron off quickly, it will begin to distort, but not shrink too fast. At this stage turn it over, place the baking parchment over and iron again. The heat will reach the raised, distorted areas first, often creating holes. The holes and bubbling combine to form amazing convoluted textures which can be sensitively adapted to look like rocks, minerals and natural, organic surfaces. These abstract textures may also provide their own inspiration.

The 'experimental' process could go on endlessly unless you keep sight of your aim of producing surfaces for stitch. These backgrounds need to reflect the quality and imagery of your source so that the stitching can marry with the surface to produce a textile where all the elements work well with each other.

(Facing page, left) This tree bark lichen effect has been achieved with a combination of materials starting with a colour-bonded ground and built up with Tyvek and expanding medium mixed with each other and painted over the undulations. The heat has been applied to the surface with a heat embossing tool, allowing a precise directing of the heat. Acrylic paint has been used as the colouring medium throughout. **Jean Littlejohn**

(Facing page, right) On a ground worked similarly to the adjacent one, some freely worked French knots and seeding stitches have been worked to 'marry' with the texture and combine tonally so that the texture is totally integrated. **Jean Littlejohn**

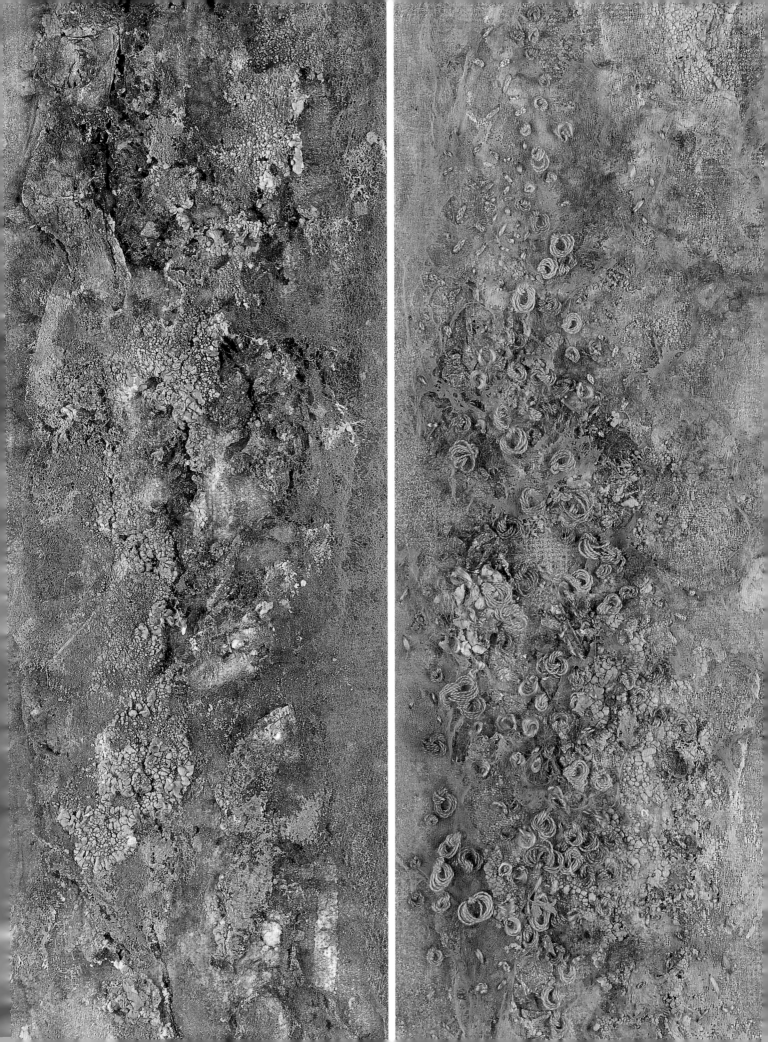

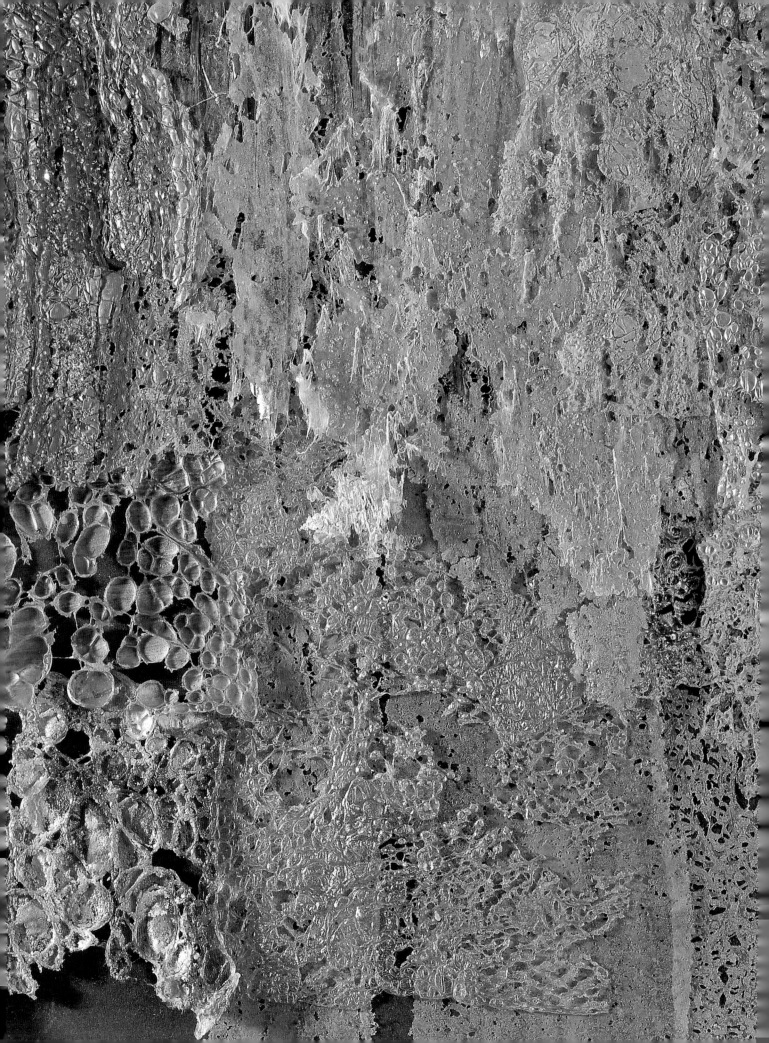

Unusual Backgrounds

Cellophane offers an alternative background material or it could be a significant part of one. It can be purchased from stationers or art and craft suppliers, but the cheapest way of obtaining it is by keeping the wrappers of paper napkins or protective coverings from books, as well as larger sheets used for wrapping flowers.

Create interesting bubbled and wrinkled surfaces by applying a hot iron to the cellophane. Sandwiching the cellophane between two sheets of baking parchment will protect the ironing surface and the base of the iron. Varying the heat settings and the length of ironing will produce an assortment of effects.

Colouring the cellophane with a range of crayons or paints can give wondrous surfaces, as the colour intensifies as the material shrinks, bubbles up or partially disintegrates. Crayons produce finer textured surfaces, whereas paint applied quite thickly produces larger raised areas. Allow time to experiment with wax crayons, iridescent paints and pastels, gouache and metallic markers. Avoid spraying the cellophane with car paints, as extremely toxic fumes rise when heat is applied. It is always a good precaution to wear a mask in a well-ventilated room when ironing a range of materials just in case they exude fumes, however slight.

Other materials layered with the cellophane will bond, adhere or be trapped within when heat is applied. Try using sequins, glitter, some metallic papers, small seeds and plant particles. Other variations will come to mind as you work. Further decorative elements can be bonded onto the cellophane and topped with chiffon which could have the dual purpose of sandwiching the additional material in place as well as slightly dulling the shine. Various foils and 'Tyvek', a type of fibrous material often used for legal documents, also distort in an interesting manner when heat is applied, and provide a bolder texture to contrast with the delicacy of some cellophane pieces. Note down all your ideas and results as accurately as possible so this knowledge can be used again at a later date. Keep your experimental pieces in a notebook.

These interesting methods of creating unusual backgrounds can look too forced unless appropriate for the surface you wish to create, so use them selectively. Fascinating surfaces produced using these ideas and applied to a conventional background could provide a sympathetic background for metal thread work and sumptuous hand stitching and beading.

This illustrates the different effects that result from applying a variety of colouring media to cellophane before the ironing process. They include iridescent and coloured oil pastels and gouache, metallic crayons and pens, acrylic paint, and pearlised airbrush colours. Some have glitter incorporated. The metallic tracery topping the samples is created by applying heat to silver foil teabag packets. Prolonged ironing lessens the silver, resulting in a subtle marbled effect. **Jan Beaney**

3

Interpreting Stitch

With the wealth of fabrics, threads and products at your disposal, it is easy to be seduced by glorious effects and forget the power of the stitched mark. With a needle and thread you can alter the surface of the cloth, make amazing patterns and affect the emotions of the viewer.

Choosing your Vocabulary

Stitching can be used to join pieces together, add strength, describe atmospheric images, decorate, enrich and adorn. The secret of successful stitching is to identify the requirement, select an appropriate stitch and find threads that will satisfy the purpose or function of the work. The careful choice of these elements will result in a stitched textile which is relevant, wholly considered, balanced and resolved. Selection of fabric and thread is also important as the quality of surface and scale of fibre will dictate the rhythm if used sympathetically.

Stitches can make wondrous textures, erupting boldly from the cloth to give dimension and scale or having such a subtle quality that they barely interrupt the surface. However, conventional constraints can so often inhibit some embroiderers. It would be thrilling if from time to time caution could be thrown to the wind and you could allow yourself time to discover the excitement and the endless creative permutations that stitched surfaces can offer. By experimenting with a range of threads as well as the scale, spacing, layering and tension of the stitch, unexpected and pleasing results can be created.

For those who are new to hand stitch, there are strategies which encourage a sensitivity to stitching. However knowledgeable, you can always learn something when carrying out stitch experiments, as you gain insight and experience every time you use a needle.

Initially two stitches, couching and detached chain, have been selected for discussion. We aim to revise, challenge and, with luck, throw off any misconceptions! Innovative variations of other stitches follow, many of which have been worked on exotic backgrounds sometimes using bizarre materials but with a strong emphasis on using them with discretion.

*This dark rich fabric could be used to make a most attractive belt or bag. Iron-on transfer fabric paints were sponged on to paper and then transferred by iron onto a cheap polyester cotton for the ground fabric. Tiny fragments of shiny, metallic fabrics and threads overlaid with sheer black chiffon were bonded onto the background. Cross stitches were then worked over this surface using a variety of yarns, including knitting tapes, silks, cottons and machine threads. Some were layered several times and others incorporate small beads in the stitching process to add textural interest. **Jan Beaney***

Couching

Couching is one of our most loved and useful stitches. It is extremely versatile and can be used to produce both delicate and bold effects. For example, pure gold threads stitched closely together, sixteen threads to each quarter inch, can be seen on the exquisite St Cuthbert's stole which dates from the tenth century which can be viewed in the crypt of Durham Cathedral. In contrast, coarser but no less exciting examples of couching can be found decorating Nigerian carnival costumes, such as those made by the Igbo tribes, where thick twists of fabric are couched into wonderful bold patterns (see page 9).

One great advantage of this stitch is that it is easy to work. Two threads are needed, one usually thicker than the other. The heavier thread is laid across the surface of the fabric in the desired position and the finer one is then used to hold it in place. In most instances the ends of the couched thread are taken through to the back of the cloth and stitched down using the thinner thread. There are, of course, exceptions to every rule and sometimes the loose ends can be darned decoratively into the front of the fabric, left to hang loosely or decorated with beads or other materials.

Couching is particularly useful because it facilitates the use of very textured, delicate or novelty threads which, if worked in conventional stitches, would be damaged as they were drawn back and forth through the fabric. Instead they can be held firmly in place by the fine thread. Heavily textured threads or their ends can be eased through to the back of the cloth using a stiletto in order to fasten on and off (see Glossary).

The wide range of embroidery, knitting, crochet and weaving tapes and yarns now available means that fascinating textures and effects (smooth, slubbed, twisted and metallic) can be achieved. Your choices may include strips of fabric, braid, ribbon, string, raffia, cords, rouleaux and strings of beads. All have their own unique characteristics. However, you can also create a wealth of exciting and unusual threads by wrapping, knotting or by adding fabric snippets, beads, and machine lace to the core yarn (see stitch diagrams on page 136). Some of these additions could provide a support structure on which to work buttonhole stitch variations and picots to introduce new textures. The only restraint is whether the embroidered item is functional or purely for decoration, because some of the above suggestions would not be suitable if the item needed to be washed.

Couching is known as a line stitch and as such the shapes of your designs can be outlined, highlighted or emphasized using long flowing lines, overlapping grids, spirals or broken lines to suggest movement. It is often referred to as the 'drawing' stitch as its linear quality can clarify or make a design 'read' more clearly. When outlining shapes, the proposed colours and textures should blend with or complement the images within the background. Such consideration will avoid a hard-edged, insensitive look to the overall design. However, if a crisp, clean-cut, hi-tech image is required, exact, precise stitching would be more appropriate.

(Facing page, above) This stitched sketch of a Canadian landscape is worked entirely in couched threads. These include torn strips of chiffon for the sky, core yarns roughly wrapped with frayed fabric and a variety of smooth threads. Fence posts and yellow stubble showing through the snow are depicted by the holding down stitch in couching (see page 35). **Jan Beaney**

(Facing page, below) A number of knotted, wrapped and textured yarns, including wool, knitting tape, raffia and torn fabric strips, have been couched into place to form a striking pattern. The threads are held in place by a variety of different stitches, some straight, some diagonal, some arranged into patterns, depending on the characteristics of the particular yarns. **Jan Beaney**

Holding Down Stitch

Another important consideration when couching is the holding down stitch. Generally, a fine thread is used where the colour and tone blends with, and does not detract from, the main yarn. Traditionally it is worked by sewing straight stitches across, and at right angles to the top thread. The stitches are spaced at regular intervals along the length of the main thread. Tight corners or circular motifs may need more closely spaced stitches to define and hold the shape. However, intriguing results and counter-rhythms can be achieved by enlarging or lengthening the holding down stitch or by working it in a discordant colour or in haphazard arrangements. Blocks of straight stitch simulating wrapped threads can also be the base for surface stitches to bead or stitch into, providing yet more exciting alternatives. Diagonal holding down stitches may be the most suitable method to couch heavily ridged twisted yarns.

As already stated, this versatile stitch can be worked in many ways. Usually, the thread lies flat against the background cloth but other textural effects can be made by looping and twisting the yarn to stand proud or protrude. This 'pendant' couching is anchored firmly in place by small stitches so as not to flatten the desired effect. Care needs to be taken that this particular look is considered within the concept of the overall design so it does not look too obvious and gimmicky.

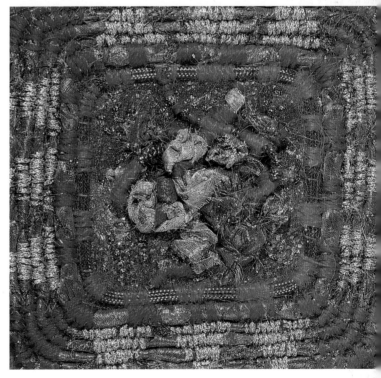

(Facing page) Bold wools and braids have been placed in a simple grid arrangement on a bonded ground, where small snippets of thread, fabric and glitter have been topped with black chiffon. Blocks of holding down stitches are featured and include silks and various metallic and faceted embroidery and crochet threads. Tiny beads have been wrapped over the main yarn as well as the holding stitch. **Jan Beaney**

(Above right) Knotted and wrapped threads have been couched down with blocks of haphazardly worked straight stitches. **Jan Beaney**

(Below right) Twists of metallic fabric placed on top of a bonded ground with gold and silk threads as holding down stitches forming a decorative pattern. Knotted and wired threads protrude from the central area. **Jan Beaney**

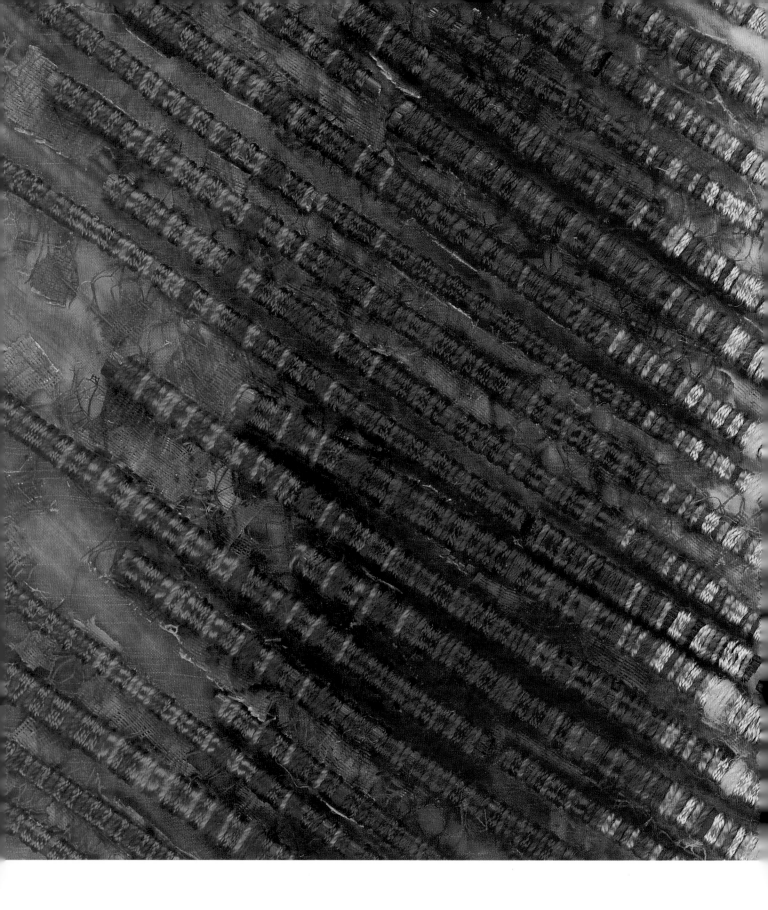

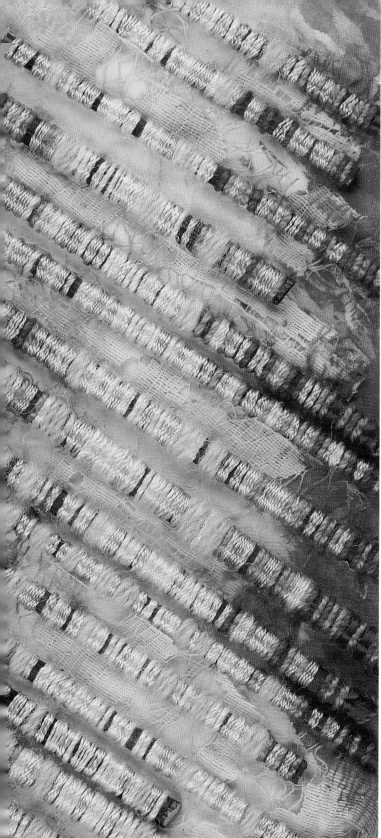

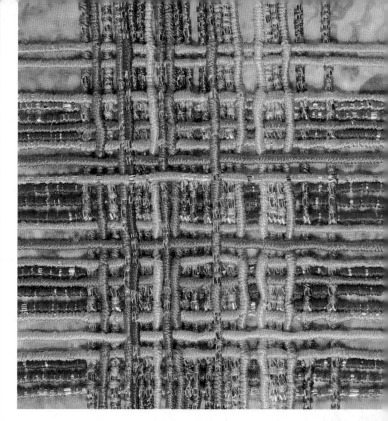

(Main picture) An excitingly vibrant piece sporting a dyed and appliquéd ground cloth, which has been decorated with lines of wooden sticks couched in a variety of matt and shiny yarns. Note how the colours have been blended one with another as well as the background. **Anne Jones**

(Above) These two pieces using square grids show layers of bright green and red silk couched over gold threads to form intriguing grid patterns. **Anne Jones**

Laid Work

This is an alternative method of arranging threads and is an effective filling stitch. Threads are couched closely together covering an area of the required cloth. If worked in one direction and a second layer stitched on top at right angles to the original, an interesting surface can be created. Some of the horses embroidered on the Bayeux Tapestry are believed to have been worked in this way. Open laid work is where threads are couched down in a latticed or chequered arrangement with spaces allowing the ground cloth to show through. In the past, contrasting coloured cross stitches have been used to hold down the threads at each intersection. Further experiments and haphazard placements could easily be developed into a creative line of thought.

Stitch dictionaries list thorn, burden and colcha stitch as all being forms of couching. The first is where the yarn is held in place by cross stitches, the second by vertical straight stitches and the third by groups of oblique irregular straight stitches. 'Or nue' is a specialized type of couching and offers sumptuous qualities. Metal threads, usually gold, are laid closely together on the ground cloth and held in place by coloured yarns. The density of the couching down stitches can be varied to make shaded patterns or to define the design (see Gallery, page 128).

A detail from an unusual and innovative panel. Dyed scrims and linen have been applied to the ground cloth and provide a contrast to the stitched panels. Stylised flower and diamond patterns are depicted by straight stitches worked over tightly twisted muslin fabrics. Running stitches make alternative marks.
Judy Turner

(Above) Spirals of felt tops couched down with freely placed randomly dyed silks. **Jean Littlejohn**

(Facing page, above) Rumanian couching worked as a line stitch and in single units in a variety of matt and shiny threads, where some of the holding down stitches have been wrapped for textural effect. **Jan Beaney**

(Facing page, below) Bokhara couching worked in the same way as the stitch above except for the placing and angle of the holding down stitch. Some of the stitches have been layered for textural interest. **Jan Beaney**

Bokhara and Romanian Couching

Up until this point the couching samples discussed have been where two threads and needles have been used. Bokhara and Romanian couching are exceptions to this and are often overlooked. With experimentation these particular stitches can offer some amazing effects.

The yarn is placed on the ground fabric to the desired length and the thread is taken through to the back of the fabric (like a long straight stitch) re-emerging a little space back in order to overstitch the line in place. Romanian couching is stitched with long oblique stitches and Bokhara with short slanting stitches with a small space between. Although effective and quick to sew, generally only straight lines and gentle curves can be achieved. Alternatively they can be worked as short stitches rather like uneven cross stitches and can be layered to create an interesting surface.

As with all the couching variations, wrapping, beading, darning or additional stitching can further embellish and develop the textural qualities. If you devote time to 'play' with these stitches, unique interpretations can be developed.

Remember

- that before commencing the stitching, the main thread is eased through from the wrong side of the cloth leaving a short end at the back. This is fastened securely in place with tiny stitches sewn with the finer needle and thread. This thread is then taken through to the right side of the cloth in order to couch the main yarn in place to form the desired pattern. On completion of the stitching, both threads are taken through to the back again and the end of the core yarn is stitched neatly in place before trimming off any excess threads.

- to keep the top thread pulled taut as you stitch in order to keep the lines flowing smoothly if desired.

- to choose a suitable background cloth. A delicate fabric, for example, will pucker if heavy cords are couched on to it. A backing fabric would eliminate the problem.

- that it can be helpful if the ends of twists of fabric are temporarily secured by a kitchen or garden wire tag to limit unravelling during the couching process.

- to keep an open mind on the types of materials that can be couched down. They could include plastic tubes, wire, wood, feathers, dried plant stems, straws and metal coils and strips. Craft shops, garden centres and DIY stores may well stock interesting variations.

Detached Chain

Couching is acknowledged as a highly versatile stitch capable of infinite variety, whereas detached chain, or 'lazy daisy', does not initially offer such promising possibilities. It is a stitch with so many associations that it is almost impossible for us to think about it without conjuring up images of tablecloths – colourful, uniform flowers with satin stitch centres and regularly spaced petals adorn countless tablecloths and placemats. All this, however, is to do it an injustice, as it is a wonderfully versatile member of the chain stitch family.

An 'isolated' stitch , it has a distinctive pattern, capable of being worked in a formal or informal arrangement. There are two parts to the stitch, the chain and the holding down stitch, both of which can be exaggerated. The holding down stitch may be lengthened or shortened and the chain may be loose, elongated or stubby and round. Using fine threads gives the stitch movement and atmosphere and with chunky threads dramatic heaps of stitches can be piled high in cones of texture. Used as a couching stitch, it gives a decorative element to the couched thread. It may also be used in concentrated blocks where the structure of the stitch is lost in the overall texture. Scattering it in a random arrangement is useful when integrating and blending. Unlike couching when you can choose to use a huge range of textured yarns, stitching here is most effective with a smooth thread for ease of working. Having said that, there are many thread varieties to use with this stitch, from the finest silk, to plastic threads and torn fabrics (see stitch diagrams on page 137).

When experimenting with this stitch there are a number of basic strategies to bear in mind:

- work the stitch by varying the scale, direction, height and width.
- work the stitches in straight lines or in circular movements.
- try rows of stitches which alternate between being the right way up and upside down.
- see how high you can pile the stitches on top of each other (after the base layer they need not go back through the fabric).
- work a row of touching stitches and then, on the next row, tuck the stitches into the first row without leaving background spaces.

*The linen ground for this piece, Turkey Series: Rose Evening, was printed with permanent fabric paint before being built up with bonded fabric scraps and a framework of couched bound pipe cleaners. Machine stitching was used to secure the work and straight stitches used to integrate and blend. To interpret the style of Turkish decoration, detached chain was used to flow into and over the couched shapes as a focus for the hand stitch. **Jean Littlejohn***

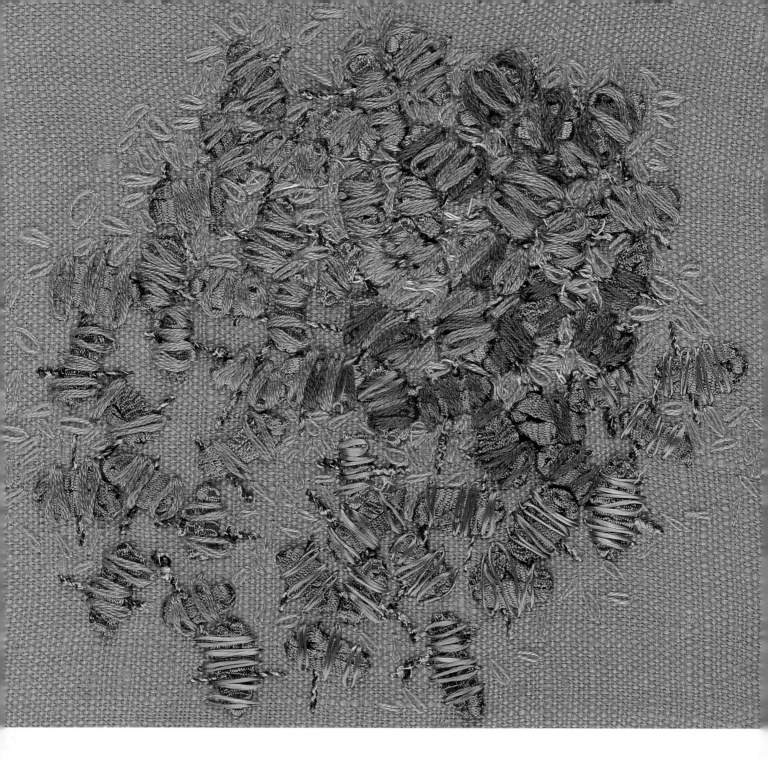

Shown here are two examples illustrating the versatility of detached chain. The piles of stitches worked in groupings have formed a texture which exploits an unconventional approach to this stitch. Worked in different directions, the establishing stitches form the base for the next layer which are worked at right angles, giving a padded appearance. The bold pattern (see facing page) does not initially look like detached chain. The couched threads are large pipe cleaners which have been wrapped with wool tops. These shapes have been secured by detached chain worked at right angles to the couched line. This offers an interesting alternative to the usual 'holding down' stitches. The pattern is fairly uniform, demonstrating that a regular pattern can incorporate innovative elements. Once more, our knowledge of stitched textiles from other cultures reminds us that it has always been acceptable to use unusual materials when available as long as they are incorporated with sensitivity.

Bundles of detached chain worked as a textured mark look effective on a contrasting ground. **Hillary Parkinson**

Large pipe cleaners were wrapped with wool tops before being couched down with detached chain stitches. **Jean Littlejohn**

When selecting stitches, we continually advise thinking beyond the stitches you feel comfortable with, but there are times when the detached chain stitch seems the obvious choice. The bookcover shown above illustrates how it enhances a highly decorative surface. The background is a patterned synthetic velvet with a rather unsubtle appearance. The idea was to treat the velvet to produce a contemporary bejewelled look. In complete contrast, the evocative piece on the facing page shows how understated this stitch can look. The fine mark offers a visual counterpoint to the matt background without disturbing the momentum of the work.

(Facing page) Coloured Bondaweb ironed onto a synthetic velvet background subdued the surface before gold heat foil was applied. A soldering iron etched through this surface to reveal the ground in places and dimensional paint highlighted areas to echo the pattern. Detached chain stitched into the surface using a shiny, synthetic thread provided the finishing touch for this very ornate fabric design conveying fading splendour. **Jean Littlejohn**

(Above) In complete contrast, this felted piece based on pathways shows a rich but subtle texture with small detached chain stitches worked to interrupt the surface and add glinting highlights. **Valerie Quay**

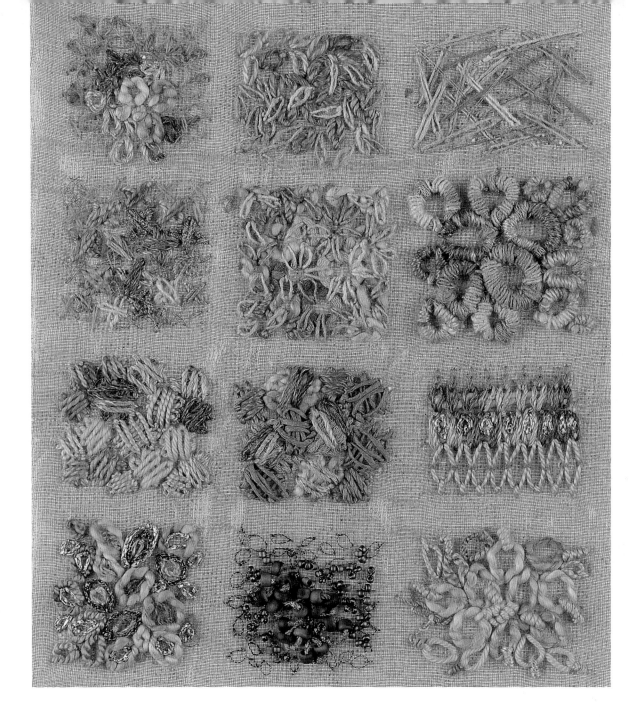

Despite being such a maligned stitch, detached chain can offer many delightful patterns or textural surfaces. Varying the amount of fabric picked up by the needle during the formation of the stitch can produce contrasting shapes, such as plump roundish stitches and long double-lined marks. Changing the thread tension will also influence the appearance. Building up several stitches one on top of the other as single units or in blocks gives intriguing effects, quite unlike the patterns usually associated with detached chain. The samples exploring the potential of this stitch shown here may inspire you to look beyond the usual, predictable stitching technique and give it another chance.

(Above) Detached chain is extremely versatile. By varying the spacing, tension, layering and the amount of fabric picked up in the stitching process, a range of textural marks can be created providing a useful reference for future work. **Jan Beaney**

(Facing page) This free interpretation of water bubbles was created with pieces of distorted cellophane, coloured with oil pastels, bonded to a photocopied image and transferred to a cotton cloth. The surface is embellished with loosely formed detached chain in cottons, silks and metallic yarn in a variety of thicknesses. **Jan Beaney**

Twisted Chain

Twisted chain is a linear stitch with a knotted texture and is another versatile member of the chain stitch family. It offers an interesting alternative to couching when working with textured lines. When used with bold threads, it produces a knobbly line, providing a textured structure. Alternatively, with a fine thread, the twisted knot is barely visible. Worked in blocks it has more body than equivalent groups of straight stitches and when built up in layers it can reflect natural forms such as minerals (see page 73).

The samples on this page are stitch experiments based on squares, where the twisted chain has been worked horizontally, vertically and diagonally on a contrasting ground for impact. Simple grid structures based on squares, triangles or lines offer good opportunities for exploiting stitch patterns. Twisted chain is a useful descriptive stitch for landscapes and seascapes – it echoes the linear rhythms and distance can be indicated by diminishing the scale and tone of the thread. Twisted chain is used in the sample on the facing page using fine metallic and silk threads to enrich the background and add lustre. Straight stitch was the first and most predictable choice here, where the design is based on a decaying Byzantine mosaic, but the irregularly worked blocks of twisted chain give a less regular line and seemed more in keeping with the spirit of the work.

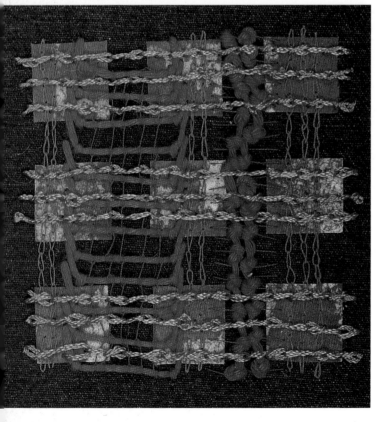

Two small samples working various chain stitches over simple bonded grids.
Hillary Parkinson

Linen painted with acrylic and printed with coloured gesso mosaic squares forms the basis for twisted chain stitch worked in a variety of threads.
Jean Littlejohn

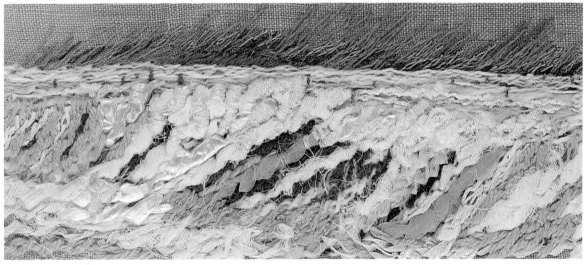

The twisted and open chain stitches illustrated here are quite versatile. They are usually considered as line stitches and can be very attractive, particularly if worked in contrasting threads, or if overlapped or layered. However, when worked as a single unit they can offer another collection of pleasing textural patterns.

(Above) Both twisted chain samples have been worked on polyester cotton where the images are printed with transfer fabric paints. The snowscapes were inspired by sketches of Canada. A wide variety of yarn materials have been used, including torn fabric strips, knitting tape, wool, silk and cotton (stitched as a line stitch and as single units, some of which are layered and wrapped). **Jan Beaney**

(Facing page) Haphazard open chain stitch worked as single units on top of cellophane applied to a fabric ground, thread snippets and sheer black chiffon. **Jan Beaney**

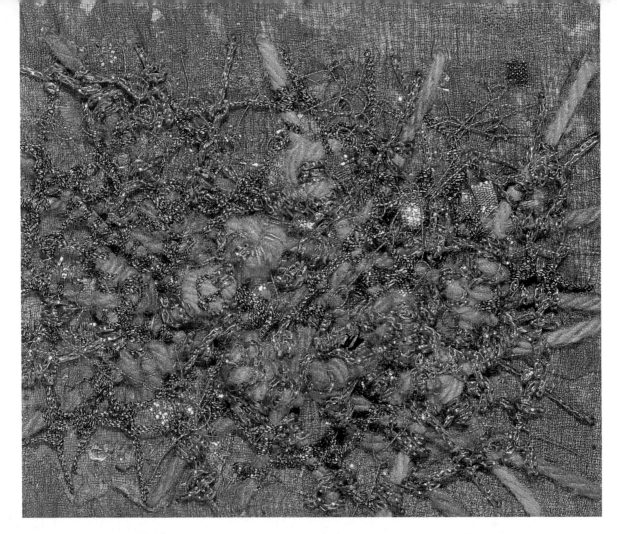

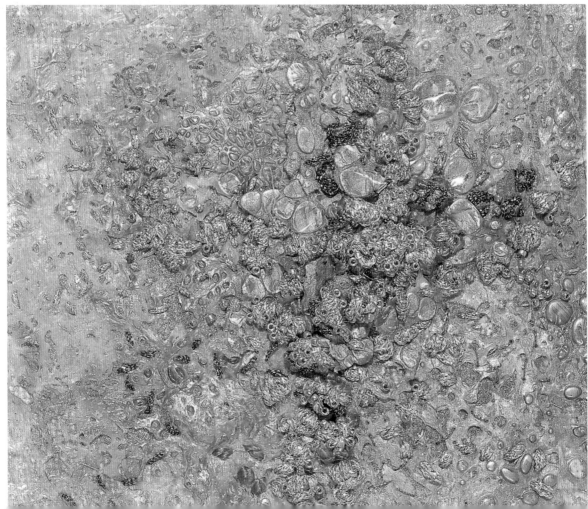

Raised Chain Band

Once mastered, the raised chain band becomes a firm favourite.
Traditionally taught as a line stitch, it provided a bold outline for
a design. It is a composite stitch – bars of straight stitch are
worked first to give a base for the chain part on top. The size and
placing of these initial bars of thread can drastically influence the
resulting surfaces in exciting ways. Short, haphazard seeding
stitches can be developed to form useful lumpy effects, or chain
stitches set over longer stitches can create a variety of networks.
The sumptuous surfaces shown here are created with fine yarns
partnered with thicker ones or layered into pinnacles and
encrusted with beads (see stitch diagram on page 132).

*(Above) Open chain stitch worked as a line stitch in a wide variety of thin and
thick threads. Inverted single stitches adorn some of the spaces and other
sections are wrapped to vary the texture.* **Jan Beaney**

*(Facing page, above) Longer support bars were criss-crossed to support the
layers of the raised chain band stitch which were worked in thick cotton,
metallic and machine threads offering contrasting effects.* **Jan Beaney**

*(Facing page, below) The ground fabric has been coloured with a metallic
paint and layered with cellophane and 'Tyvek'. Gold and silver liquid markers
were applied to both before ironing to shrink and disintegrate. Single raised
chain band stitches have been layered into pinnacles and beaded. Care was
taken to build up the texture gradually and seeding stitches help blend and
integrate into the background.* **Jan Beaney**

Cretan Stitch

This is a reliable favourite in a stitch vocabulary. According to the amount of fabric picked up in the needle, it can be worked as a formal line stitch and in close blocks it provides a filling stitch. In traditional Cretan embroidery, the stitches worked in brightly coloured silks were arranged into ornate borders of complex patterns. Cretan stitches can produce long, irregular and elegant rhythms which evoke swaying grasses in the breeze. The stitch has a simple structure where the threads cross, and is invaluable in that it gives an 'anonymous' look. Infinite variations will emerge when layering the stitches, and changing the threads, colours and direction.

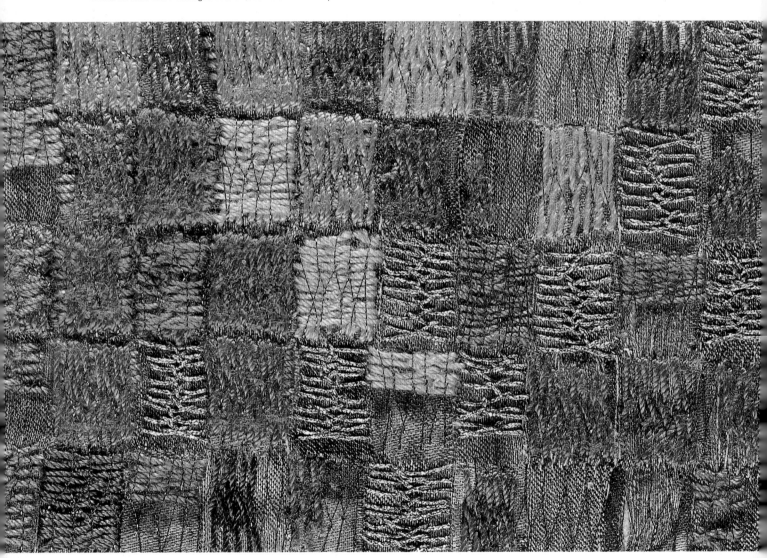

(Above) A synthetic metallic woven fabric ironed with a transfer print provides a background for a semi-formal use of Cretan stitch, worked vertically and horizontally to echo water patterns. The stitches gradually build up in layers towards the base. **Jean Littlejohn**

(Facing page) Free Cretan stitch echoes the circular scales inspired by the skin of a lizard. The ground is heat-expanding medium painted with acrylic. **Jean Littlejohn**

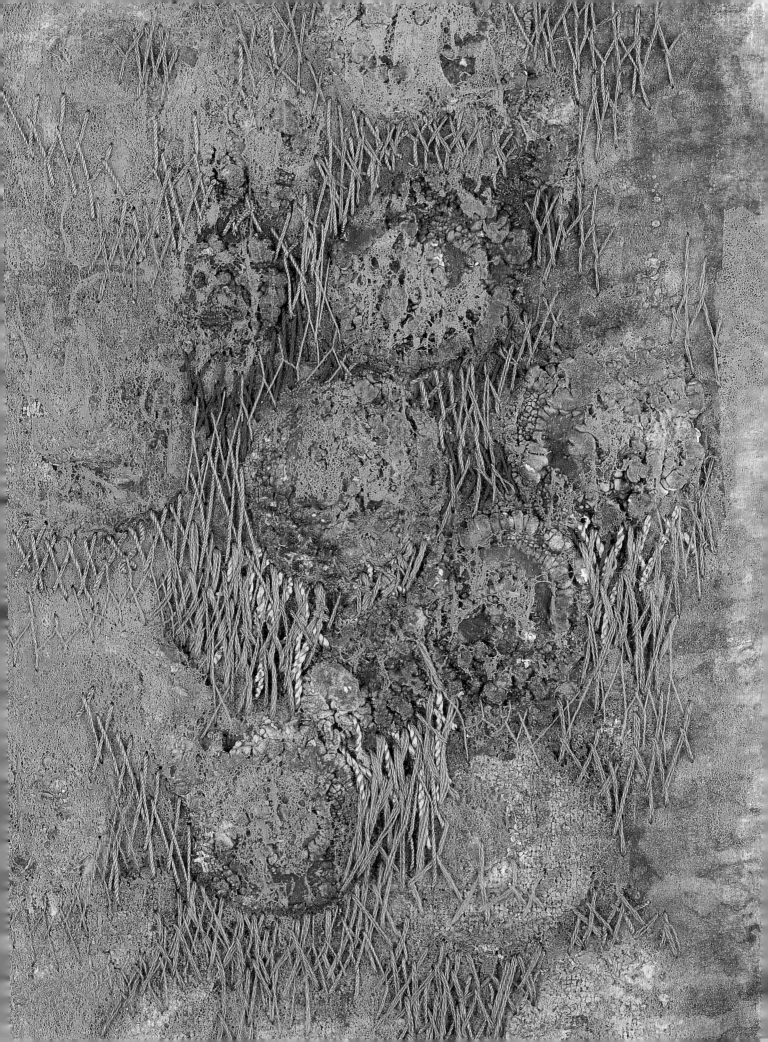

Cross Stitch

Cross stitch worked with one thread is often used in a regular way for covering canvas or forming a geometric design on evenweave linen. It can also be tremendously exciting, particularly when worked in a range of threads. Encrusted surfaces can be created by layering and beading the stitches, or rhythmic linear patterns may suggest grassy or plant-like marks. Alternatively, smaller cross stitches worked in clusters or drifts blend and integrate colours and shapes within the background. This stitch is featured in the stitch diagram on page 132.

(Above) Layers of cross stitches were worked in a striped arrangement, the shiny threads and beads decorating the main area of interest. **Jan Beaney**

(Facing page, above) This sample demonstrates one of the sections being the focal point where the layers of stitch are higher and adorned with beads. **Jan Beaney**

(Facing page, below) The area of interest is more central and the threads nearer the outside edge are finer. Notice that all examples have colour drifts running throughout the piece in varying degrees, to link and integrate. **Jan Beaney**

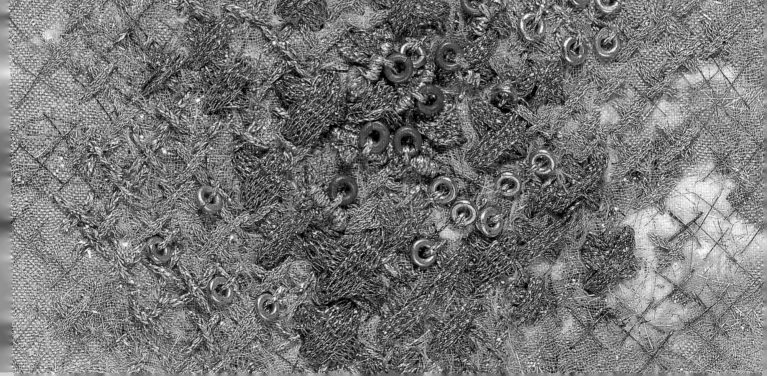

Buttonhole Stitch

The basic interpretation of this stitch has long been used for edging functional items, such as blankets or buttonholes, when the stitches are worked close together. It is a remarkably versatile stitch and has many variations besides the freely worked networks that can be improvised. Worked in rows, it forms angular structures and formal patterns. Altering the length, width and direction liberates it from its traditional form, and makes it possible to explore fluid waves of texture and colour. Fine threads which are sympathetic to the ground fabric also enable buttonhole stitch to be used for subtle blending and interacting. The many variations include knotted, detached and tailor's buttonhole stitch, all of which have individual characteristics and can be used to create different effects. Buttonhole bars and detached buttonhole rings can be built layer upon layer into encrusted and enriched surfaces.

(Facing page) The vibrant Indian textile pictured here really highlights the bold and dramatic qualities of hand stitch. Buttonhole has been used very effectively to emphasise the flower and leaf patterns. It makes a strong and simple mark within the composition and underlines the sheer exuberance of hand stitching.

(Below) An Egyptian eye motif worked as a repeat pattern has been the source of inspiration for this feast of buttonhole stitches in different thicknesses, scales and directions. **Tanya Pannell**

Knots

There are a number of stitches with knotted characteristics, but the most popular one must be the French knot. It has been used extensively in conventional embroideries as an isolated stitch or in clusters. If placed insensitively it can look spotty and disjointed, but is most effective in rich, textured surfaces (see next spread). Worked accurately, it forms a compact circular pattern and the stitch process is a satisfying one. When worked 'badly' it loops and distorts, often creating interesting effects, but working it this way can be more difficult and does take practise.

Keep the thread slack when winding it through the needle to produce exotic little looped knots and for large knots, use thicker threads. Although less often used, bullion knots look really good when distorted. The traditional technique involves wrapping a thread around a core stitch and the resulting stitch then resembles a caterpillar. To produce distortion in this small piece, the stitch needs to be elongated and the thread wrapped a few times to create a linear rippled effect.

(Facing page) The plastic background of this piece supports a delicate structure where leaves and fragments have been trapped and bonded between two layers of painted Bondaweb. After the paper was peeled back, chiffon was ironed over the surface to give support (with a covering of baking parchment to protect it while being ironed). Delicate buttonhole stitches have been worked in random rhythms to add movement. **Jean Littlejohn**

(Above) Transfer printed image embellished with open buttonhole. Some parts of the stitch have been wrapped and beaded. **Jan Beaney**

(Facing page) Distorted Bullion knots worked on a cotton ground with acrylic painted Bondaweb ironed on to evoke a seascape. **Jean Littlejohn**

(Above) This free interpretation of seed heads has been worked as a single stitch in a distorted knotted buttonhole. The background features looped French knots. **Christine Habib**

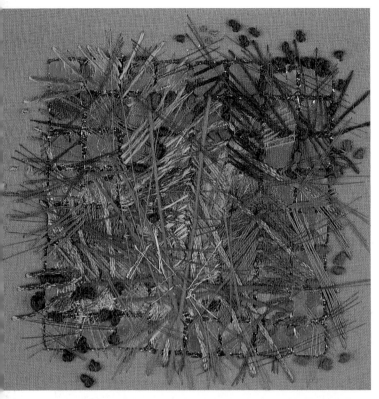

Straight Stitch

The two straight stitch interpretations illustrated here show just how dynamic and versatile this simple stitch can be, creating effects ranging from dramatic to sensitive. Their lack of intricacy also allows them to be used interpretively and anonymously.

(Left) Straight stitches worked freely and in different directions over an applied ground. **Hillary Parkinson**

(Below) Straight stitches in simple, loosely worked linear rhythms, displaying looped textures. **Anne Jones**

(Facing page) The straight stitches in this piece have been worked over a complex ground of bonded appliqué on paper with hand and machine stitching. Because of the varied elements, the straight stitches help to co-ordinate and simplify the image as well as highlight the lettering. **Jean Littlejohn**

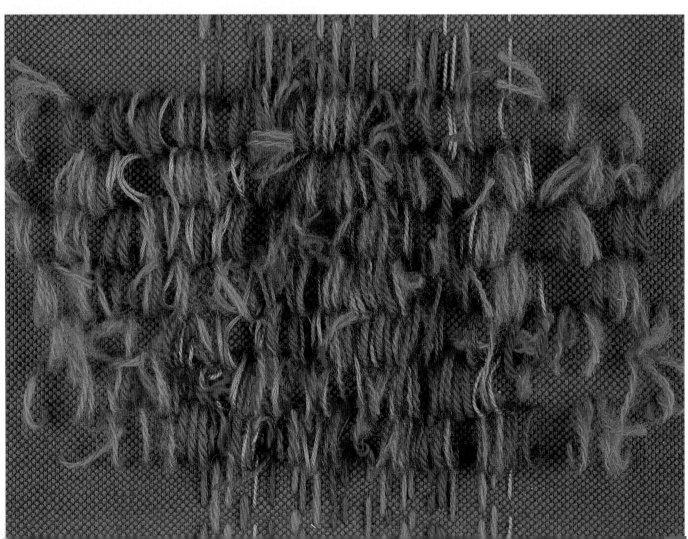

Building Stitches

Stitch may be totally absorbed and integrated into the fabric of the ground as in darning, yet it still gives an extra dimension of surface. Most stitching involves creating another level of surface on the cloth. However, there are times when an even greater dimension of surface is required and there are various ways to achieve this.

Stitching has the amazing capacity to contort into heavily raised and undulating areas where the work requires. For some large-scale pieces of work the quality and scale of the mark needs to be enlarged to give the weight and contrast to the piece. Raised textures on wall hangings cast shadow and add an exciting dynamic to the piece.

Stitching into Frameworks

Stitching most often occurs on relatively flat areas but there are times when a prepared raised framework can offer an extra dimension. Padding, applied textures and fabric manipulation can offer such possibilities. Wire, drinking straws, pipe cleaners and other devices can also be employed to produce raised areas and have a valid place in the embroiderer's vocabulary. Pipe cleaners may be bought in a range of colours and thicknesses and bound or wrapped to good effect. They combine the bending properties of wire with the softness of fibre.

To incorporate such frameworks into a piece of work, it is first necessary to identify the underpinning structure of the piece. For example, in an architectural piece, such as a moulded pattern, the basic shapes can be couched with raised ridges, maybe using wrapped pipecleaners. Having established the basic framework, the stitches may be worked over and into the framework to fully integrate it into the background. To achieve a harmonious effect it is necessary to pay particular attention to the tonal values. Less regular textures, such as tree bark, may also have a basic structure which can be laid down and then further stitches added to give an extra dimension.

PVA glue, when mixed with water, can be used successfully to manipulate fabric textures. This is best achieved by supporting the glued fabric on a plastic sheet and manipulating or combining pieces until the desired effect has been gained and then allowing it to dry. It may be peeled off the plastic and applied to the ground fabric. Although one part glue to two parts water is a good guide, the less glue used the more pliable the surface. Having prepared a framework and secured it to the ground, further stitching may be worked over and around.

There is a tendency to stop at ridges when stitching, but it can be most effective to carry on working over lumps and bumps where appropriate, so the raised areas emerge from the cloth and integrate with the image.

Kalami, Water Levels shows how a range of layers have been worked on a printed linen ground to achieve the look of the ever-changing patterns and networks under the sea. Silk threads knotted into structures on wooden frames were painted with a watered down solution of PVA glue and then couched down in layers, trapping starfish and other shapes within. The flexible grid on top was made from pipe cleaners, joined into a network and wrapped with torn silk. This network still moves and echoes the changing water patterns as the tides ebb and flow. Having established the layers of grids, surface stitches were worked in and out of the structures.
Jean Littlejohn

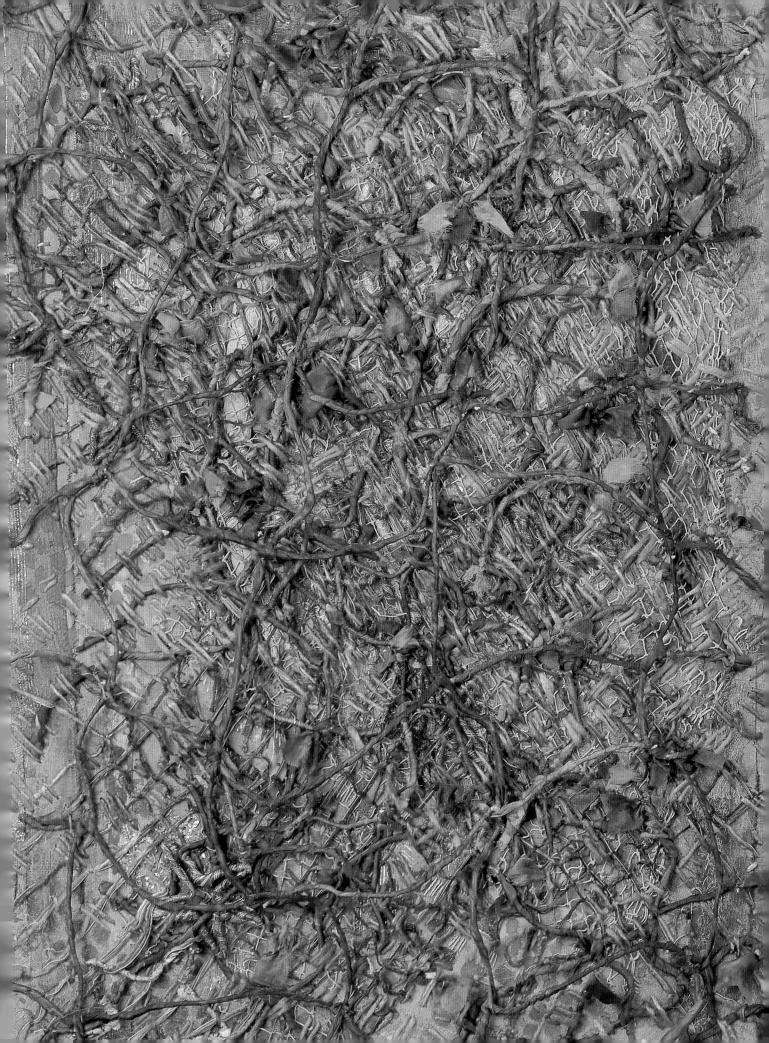

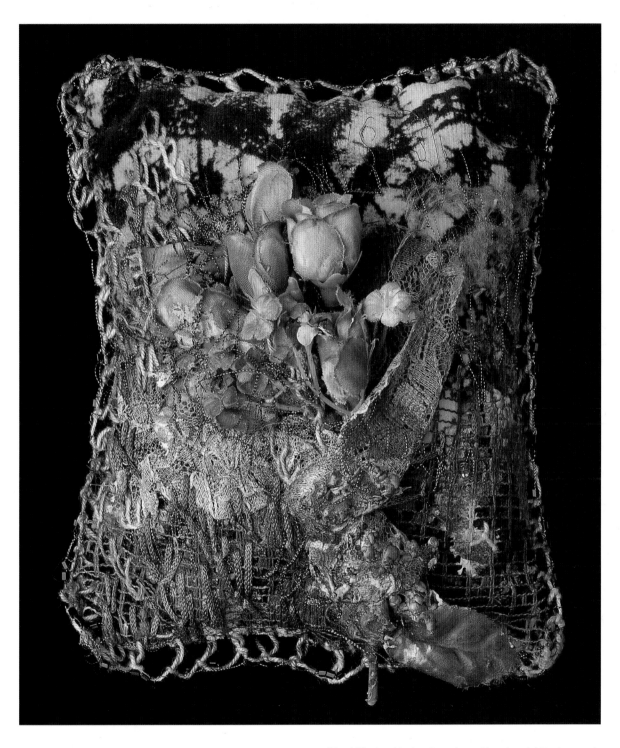

(Facing page) The structure supporting the stitches on this old tile piece has been made from stiffened and manipulated bandage gauze. The plastic was painted with a watered down mix of PVA. Gauze was applied and strips manipulated into the surface, adding glue where necessary. When the texture dried, this was peeled off the backing and applied to a printed black background before working free cross stitch in and over the texture to integrate it with the ground. **Jean Littlejohn**

(Above) This pincushion based on a theme of 'arsenic and old lace' was made from 'discharged' black velvet and nylon lace. The synthetic flowers have been subdued with a wash of acrylic paint and stitched onto the surface. The textured expanding medium, coloured with a wash of acrylic paint, has been painted over the flowers to complete the distressed look. This complex ground forms the basis for buttonhole stitch worked in and over the structure and is finished with a knotted buttonhole beaded edging to reinforce the 'Victorian' feel. **Jean Littlejohn**

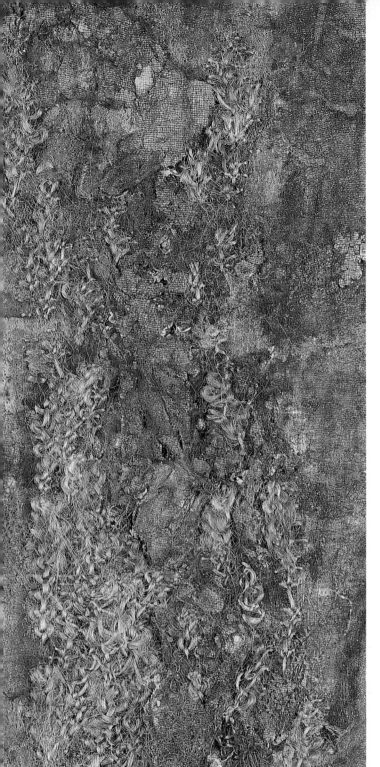

Piles of Stitches

The full value of stitch can be seen when making piles or towers of stitches with no added support. Surprising results are possible.

For raised textured areas, stitches with a structure are particularly useful. The chain stitch family can be worked most effectively in formal, semi- formal or chaotic constructions which emerge from the background. Detached chain can lose its tightness when worked in pyramid-like features or less regular organic forms. Twisted chain gives possibilities for linear structures with raised areas. Raised chain band, worked stitch on stitch, offers a knotted and gnarled feel. There are very few stitches that cannot be developed in this way and tackling some unpromising candidates could provide an alternative way of working. Indeed, this is a real opportunity to find new ways of expressing yourself with stitch. Yet again, the extra vitality that an injection of innovative stitching will provide may take you over a barrier and into undiscovered stitched surfaces.

Composite Stitches

These are stitches that involve more than one working method and they are often complex. The most simple is perhaps whipped running stitch where the running stitch forms the base and the whipping takes place as a separate operation. Many stitches may be whipped or interlaced to good effect. Others, such as raised chain band, have wonderful pattern qualities when used as a line stitch but become very textural when built up layer upon layer. In this way the structure of the stitch becomes absorbed in the overall texture. By mixing fabrics and threads in a range of qualities and thicknesses infinite possibilities occur. Once the first layer has been established, subsequent stitches can be worked on top of each other without going into the ground.

(Above) Raised chain band worked in layers on a ground of coloured expanding medium with sheer chiffon on the surface. **Jean Littlejohn**

(Facing page) A holiday photograph of minerals on a dried-up river bed has been transferred to fabric from a photocopy on a film which can then be ironed off. This technique is similar to that used to print on T shirts. This forms the basis of piles and layers of twisted chain worked in a variety of threads. **Jean Littlejohn**

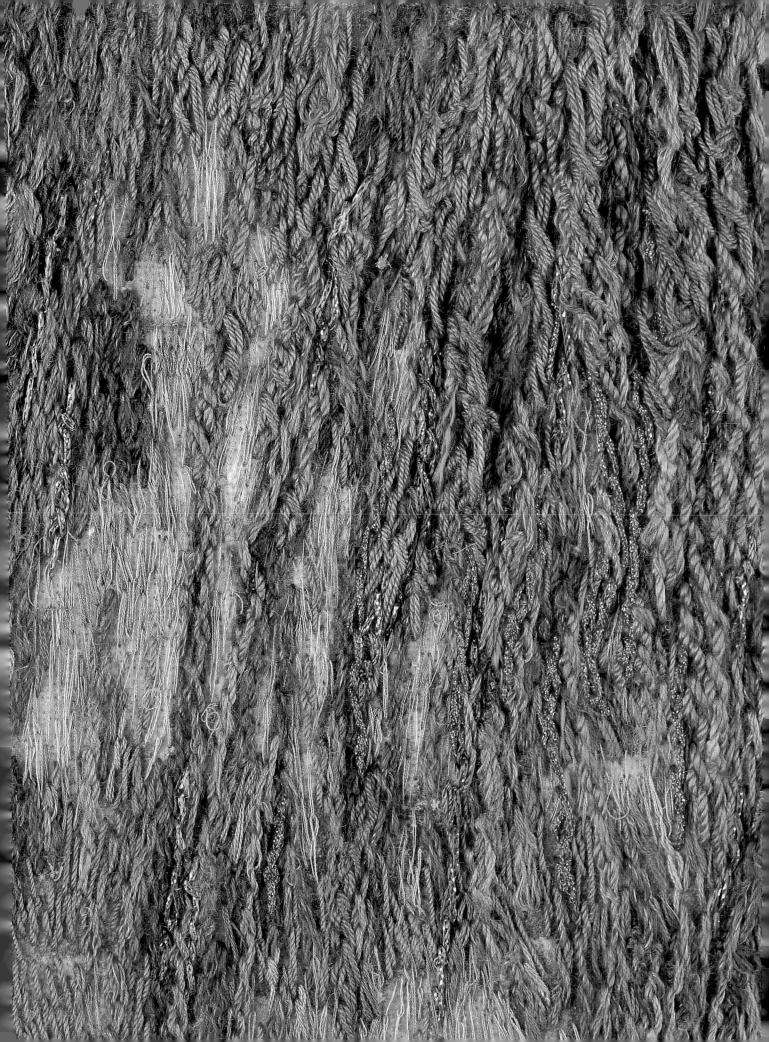

Creating Organic Dimension

The dictionary definition of 'organic' includes the terms 'give orderly structure to', 'connected', 'interdependent', 'systemic' and 'co-ordinated'. These so closely echo the rhythms of stitch structures that you can be influenced by this whole feel. This way of working could be equally described as 'trust the stitch'. Having selected a stitch which reflects the characteristic most appropriate to your source of inspiration, you need to become accustomed to the feel of the stitch and allow it to grow into the cloth. Pay close attention to the look of the stitch and note how one shape links with another. Note the background shapes and how they relate to the feel of the stitch. Try interlocking the stitch at different angles and varying the scale and direction.

Stitches that particularly suit this method include fly stitch, ladder or open chain, wave stitch and others with a rhythmic structure. To get the feel of working in this way, work the stitch in the centre of a piece of cloth and work outwards, trying to fill the spaces with the stitch as you go. This may involve revolving the work in your hands to change the direction and the scale. Remember to create a structure first, then go back and work further stitches within the structure, filling the spaces with threads in a variety of sizes and qualities.

Look out for sources in nature with 'organic' patterns which could inspire work in this way. These could include pineapples, fir cones, the centres of sunflowers, plant stems and seed heads. Reptile skins with crusty, gnarled surfaces and other animal patterning could also prove exciting starting points. Even surfaces such as tree bark, which may initially look haphazard, have an underpinning logic to their patterning which, if recognized, can provide a clue to successfully interpreting the imagery in stitch. Time spent in observing, recording and drawing these patterns will repay with the resulting heightened awareness of the logical rhythms of nature and the possibilities for stitched textiles.

(Facing page) This piece, loosely based on the patterns from the snake skin opposite, celebrates the structure of fly stitch which creates the pattern around which the rhythms are stitched. **Jean Littlejohn**

(Right) Discarded snake skin, showing the rhythmic linking patterns which could be used as a starting point for building stitches laterally.
Jean Littlejohn

Mountains and Foothills (layering stitches)

Having selected or created a suitable background, care needs to be taken to choose threads which will tone in and blend with it. The aim is to work the stitches to look as if they 'grow' out of the cloth. In the first instance, choose one stitch to feature with the possibility of including other 'helping' stitches at a later stage.

The order of working the stitches can vary. It may be helpful to cover the fabric first with very fine stitches in order for them to 'peep' through the areas of stitching to be worked later. Generally the larger stitches are blocked in first, followed by medium, small and very fine ones. It is advisable not to start layering and decorating the stitches until you are satisfied that the scale, colour and arrangement are as you intended. Following this stage, layers of stitch can be built up to varying degrees, developing interesting effects but still maintaining the general characteristics of the piece. Groups of medium-sized stitches can nestle in with bolder aspects, and smaller clusters of very fine stitchery can blend to integrate all the aspects into a coherent whole. Consider the analogy of a mountain in order to help you with the placement of the stitches: high peaks and ridges give way to lower ones before the foothills take over and merge into the undulating plains at the base of the mountain.

Built up stitches can provide a support system for others to be suspended across or as a base for alternative stitches to be formed, many of which only need a bar of thread for the first stage of working. Threads can be darned through some areas to link or provide a glint of colour or a textural variance. Wrapping, beading, tying and picots are all additions that can embellish the embroidery as long as the placements have been considered carefully so as not to make the piece too busy with isolated peaks of interest.

Remember

- when layering stitches on four or more levels, some threads may slip down and become out of place. Wrapping another yarn, or one threaded with tiny beads, around the structure will help to stabilize it. To do this, bring another thread to a position at the base of one of the 'legs' of the cross. Without stitching into the ground cloth, wrap the thread over the layered stitch from one side to the other until you have covered or partially covered it, depending on the required effect. Take the thread to the back of the cloth in order for it to re-emerge at the end of the second 'leg' of the cross.

- a limited colour scheme is recommended for working the initial placing with tonal and textural variations. Other colours can be introduced to highlight or contrast as the work progresses. Tiny amounts of complementary colours (opposite colours on the colour wheel) when sensitively placed can add verve to the piece.

This highly textured piece has been worked entirely in cross stitches in thick, thin, matt and shiny threads. Some stitches have been layered two, three, four or more times, wrapped to stabilise them and tied with fabric strips – a few are even topped with wrapped or buttonhole picots. When working a piece of this nature, remember to imagine a landscape of 'mountains and foothills'. **Jan Beaney**

4

Unifying Stitches within a Background

Integrating and merging dyed and stitched fabric or fabric shapes within an embroidery is often a challenge. There are, however, some simple stitch methods which can be used to develop a greater sensitivity and awareness in order to unify a stitched piece of work.

Integrating

Many embroiderers demonstrate excellent technical abilities and can work the most complicated stitches beautifully but find it difficult to use these skills to create a well-considered unified design. There can be too many competing focal points which may fragment the overall composition. When creating an embroidery it is essential to integrate or link shapes within their background so that the eye is led around the imagery and towards the main area of interest.

There are many ways an embroiderer can tackle the problem of unifying a stitched piece. Colour co-ordinating the threads to the ground cloth or dyeing your fabric and threads together can be helpful. Applied shapes or bonded snippets of fabric and thread can include the colour and elements of the actual thread to be used for the stitchery. For example, tiny gold filaments or glitter bonded under chiffon would be a way of linking any gold or metallic stitching. Working within a limited colour scheme need not be restricting as the shadows cast by even the finest stitching will be enough to develop the surface and can be more influential than people realize. Other colours can be introduced to mingle gently with the existing ones so as not to dominate. This approach will help you create a richly textured surface without the stitches looking as if they are added as an afterthought.

Fabric and paper pieces have been assembled to make an exciting work from which this detail is drawn. Some have been applied by machine and others by straight stitches. The tone and colouring of the additional stitches blend to form a totally integrated design. **Hilary Bower**

(Above) This richly stitched panel evokes a shimmering heat haze, where brightly dressed figures collecting water form part of the landscape. The running and straight stitches not only depict the colour of the clothing but, by encroaching onto the background fabric, help to totally integrate and blend the images within the fabric. Notice that small areas of formal pattern have been depicted to add interest without intrusion. A simple line of running stitches helps link the decorative surround to the central piece. **Jean Draper**

(Facing page, below) This dyed and bonded fabric has been worked in simple seeding, running and straight stitches to 'marry' the background and foreground by blending the edges. The colours of the thread have been changed so as to blend them sensitively with the ground cloth. **Fay Green**

Linking with Worker Stitches

'Worker' stitches are ones that do not necessarily feature prominently within the piece but do the most essential task of linking various areas throughout the work, as well as blending the images sensitively within the background cloth. They can meander in and around the images, drift through the shapes or provide a low relief to integrate with the more textural ones. Running, straight, seeding, knot, cross and other stitches worked as a single unit could be considered to do the required job effectively.

Imagine an appliquéd or stitched picture worked in satin and velvet fabrics and with lustrous yarns. To add interest, isolated shapes of rough scrim or coarse thread have been randomly placed, but these look far too obvious and are extremely mismatched. The predominance of these elements may be lessened and successfully merged with the background if fragments of these materials were mingled in with the main elements. Fraying or distressing the edges to blend in or overlap and using worker stitches to drift through and around are both methods for blending the shapes into a workable composition. Similarly if a coloured shape or stitch is too prominent, link it with the background by using tiny lines, specks or drifts of stitching in a similar colour, or one that has slightly less impact, in order for it to tone in.

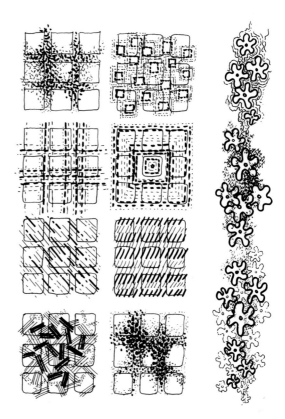

(Above) The two left strips show ways of positioning stitched marks in order to integrate the shapes. The worker stitches could include variations of cross, straight, single, knot or chain stitches.

The right strip with the stylised flower border shows three ways to blend the shapes within the background. Firstly with lines echoing the main shapes and also with clusters or drifts of stitches mingling around and through the shapes. The lower section illustrates the addition of less defined flower motifs, plus dot marks to integrate the whole design.

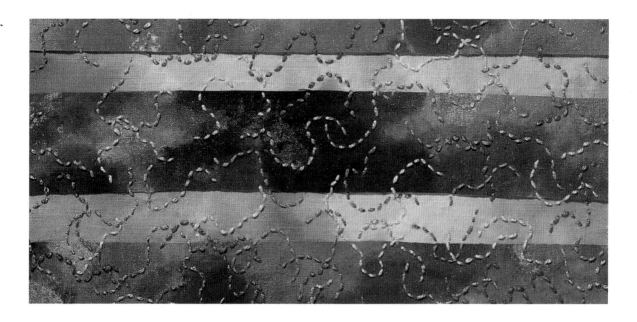

Growing from the Cloth

Sumptuous, exciting effects can be achieved by layering and overlapping stitches to form an encrusted surface. However, care must be taken to give the impression that the stitches have grown out of the ground cloth. To achieve this, the tone, colour and texture of thread should be considered and time taken to build up the stitches gradually from the background. As already suggested, equating this layered effect to the different levels of a mountain may help you to decide how and where to build up and emphasize the stitchery for greatest effect. Isolated clumps of unrelated bold stitchery can look unattractive, so always allow the textures to flow, following imaginary contours.

To help you identify features within a design source you have selected, whether it is the actual subject or a photograph, a number of observational exercises can be practised. After a little experience they could help improve your looking, drawing, design and stitching skills. Natural forms, textural surfaces or the countryside may be your chosen area of interest, as organic characteristics are suitable for sympathetic interpretation in fabric and thread.

Initially choose a photograph or sketch. Using a paper frame or 'L' shapes, select an area out of context, trying a variety of positions before making a final decision. Commence by placing your finger at the top edge and follow any dark shapes that run down and through the whole area. Then repeat the procedure to see if any similar tones or shapes run (even in a meandering way) from side to side. Having already marked out the boundary of the design, make quick sketches in your notebook indicating these main shapes only, without details. If you find that you become too involved with small unconnecting shapes, place the reference further away from you and half close your eyes when viewing it. In most cases you will then become aware that darker tones are much simpler in shape and do link, albeit tenuously, at some points. It is these shapes that will form the underlying foundation of your piece, giving it a unified and integrated feel. At times several shapes will appear unrelated. Intensifying your observation will most probably reveal some colours or texture links not initially apparent. Repeat the exercise but select a colour or a textural feature, and trace their position or placements down through and across the picture. These elements should be noted down before embarking on the design for the stitched piece. It is these subtle observations of colour drifts which will influence the unity of the work. Some features can be understated or emphasized in order to develop an original image and also to link all the parts within the whole (see example on pages 86–7).

The list overleaf includes some recommendations from our previous books which are still relevant. As basic design considerations, they are not a passing fashion. They may be useful reminders to help you to create stitchery that 'sits' happily within the work. Obviously some suggestions will apply more than others.

*These delightful tiny darned pictures feature appliquéd animals. The shapes have been sensitively blended within their backgrounds by darning over the fabric edges and also at times into and over the shape. **Phil Palmer***

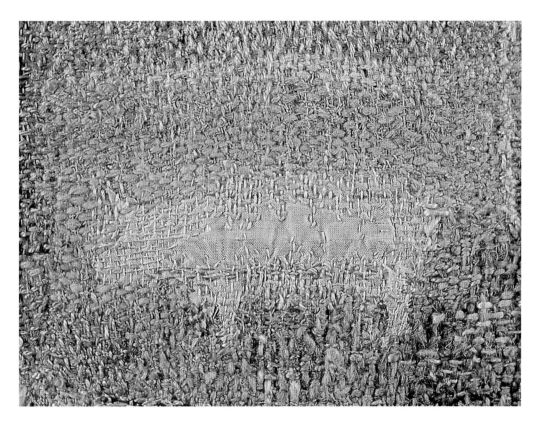

Remember

- that fabric edges can be distressed or frayed to soften them and blend them into the background cloth.
- that stitches can be worked on the edges of applied fabrics to break across the main lines of the design.
- to ensure the fabric pieces or stitches tone with or complement the ground cloth.
- that drifts or clusters of tiny textural stitches can be used to encroach, entwine, mingle within and link shapes together
- in general, certain colours and textures need to be reflected throughout the work without being predictable. Avoid using equal amounts of an aspect resulting in a bland image.
- to place tiny snippets of the yarn on the cloth to ascertain the right colours and tones of threads to blend within a background. Looking through half-closed eyes will enable you to judge if colours are too light, dark or bright as this will make them 'jump out' discordantly. Unless this is part of your concept, this exercise is always useful but is so often forgotten. When using a discordant colour scheme to shock the viewer, consider it carefully to keep the work unified.
- the power of the thread – as it can seduce and confuse. Shiny, twisted threads reflect the light and, if placed thoughtlessly, could set up another focal point. Matt threads, however, tend to recede. In general, warm colours and very dark and light tones can dominate. Be aware of their strength and consider whether they are working well in their setting or if they need to be toned down. If necessary this could be rectified by additional fabric, dye or stitch to help these areas sit well within the work.

Two experimental pieces where the background fabrics were coloured with fabric paints and then bonded with snippets of metallic fabrics, threads and sheers to make interesting surfaces. Cloth strips and padded rouleaux were then couched onto the backgrounds to create these richly textured samples. Notice how the colours of the couched threads have been carefully chosen to blend in with the background. **Anne Jones**

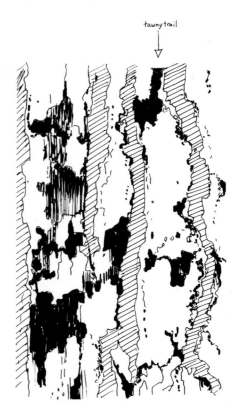

tawny trail

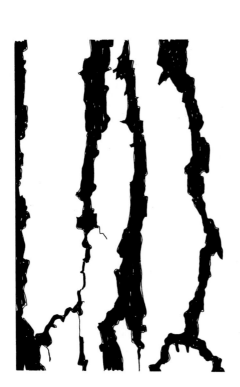

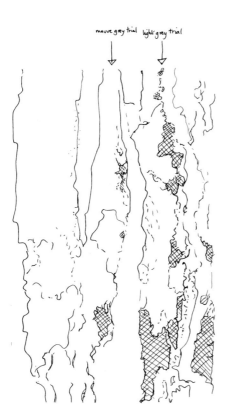

mauve grey trial   light grey trial

(Above left) This shows a rough plan marking out the dark-toned shapes of the photograph opposite which give an underlying structure to the piece.

(Above right) A first glance at the photograph, the large orange, tawny coloured patches look isolated, but by following the trail with your finger, starting at the top of the coloured picture, you will see that smaller areas of specks or dots link nearly all the shapes. This diagram indicates these observations.

(Left) The same principle applies to the very light areas – follow the trail meandering from main shape to fine line down and across the picture. This exercise will improve your observation of more subtle colourings, and should also influence how you position the stitches, providing a linking mechanism to unify the piece. This also means that you are less likely to create a 'busy' composition with too many areas competing with each other.

(Facing page) A section of tree bark, providing inspiration for embroidery. Consider the tonal qualities by looking at the coloured picture through half-closed eyes and notice that the bark areas with the tawny, mauve-grey and very light sections tend to be very close in tone. When working from your own photographs, remember to follow this procedure as some colours and tones may not be the same tonal value as your initial impression. The crevices appear very dark, but they are only a darker version of the tree trunk colour. Due to surrounding colour reflections, it is unusual to use pure black or white when interpreting observations from natural sources.

Jan Beaney

Blending

When you need to blend areas sensitively within a composition, there are various stitches which prove useful and these include the whole straight stitch family. Seeding, running stitches, groups of straight stitches in increasing or diminishing size and thickness can carry a rhythm, and 'marry' appliqué or surface additions into the background. Free cross stitch can be used very successfully to work rhythmic and dramatic movements as well as subtle blending. There are strategies for acquiring the skill which may be worked quite simply (see captions on facing page).

Points for Consideration

The tone and quality of the thread is most important to the success of this method. Select threads which echo the colours of the shapes to be blended. An alternative, but equally effective, method is to take the colour from the ground and 'run' it into the shape to be integrated so that the ground and the applied areas become a whole cloth.

Stranded threads are very useful because they can be diminished from six, to five, to four threads, and so on, giving a simple blending method. Also to achieve colour gradation, colours can be mixed in the needle. To work smoothly from blue to green, work six blue threads in the needle, followed by five blue and one green thread, then four blue and two green and continue until six green ones are being used.

Machine embroidery threads used to blend almost invisibly into the ground work very well. Shaded threads may prove a useful addition but always look at the range of tones, as an excessively light or dark tone within the thread may interrupt the fluidity. Imagine ripples on a pond; when a stone is cast, the ripples are concentrated and closer together and they gradually fade as they work out towards the edges.

Used sensitively, French knots, and buttonhole or blanket stitch in its various forms can blend and integrate beautifully, bearing in mind the considerations listed above.

Working in this way, selecting an outwardly unpromising stitch and exercising the full scale range from almost invisible to richly textured, may not only look stunning but will almost certainly inspire future textiles.

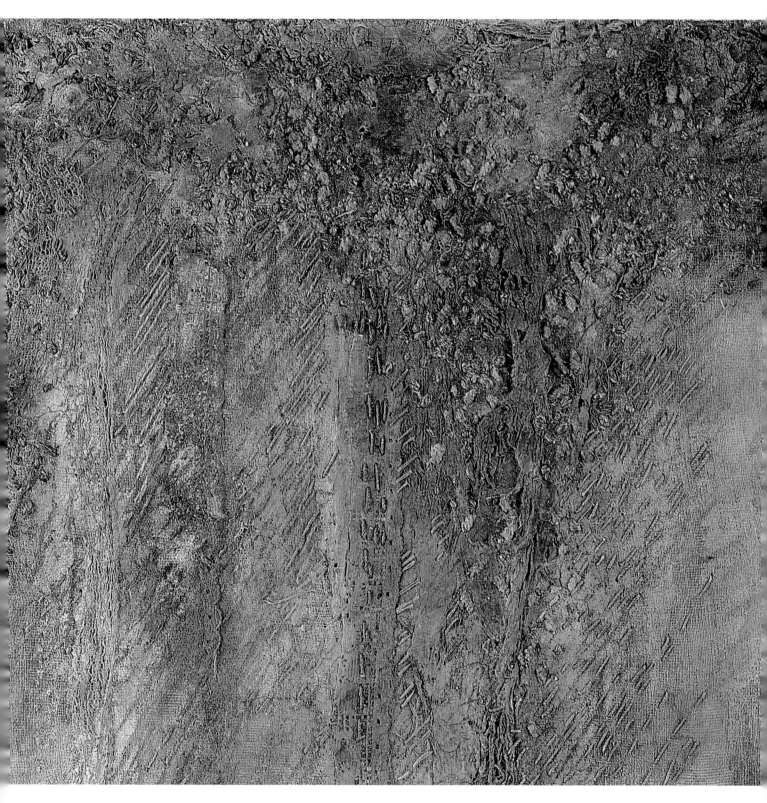

(Facing page) This sample shows the use of seeding, running and straight stitches to 'marry' the background and foreground by blending the edges.
Jean Littlejohn

(Above) The background of this piece incorporates lace and gesso, painted with acrylic wax before using seeding and running stitches to add movement.
Jean Littlejohn

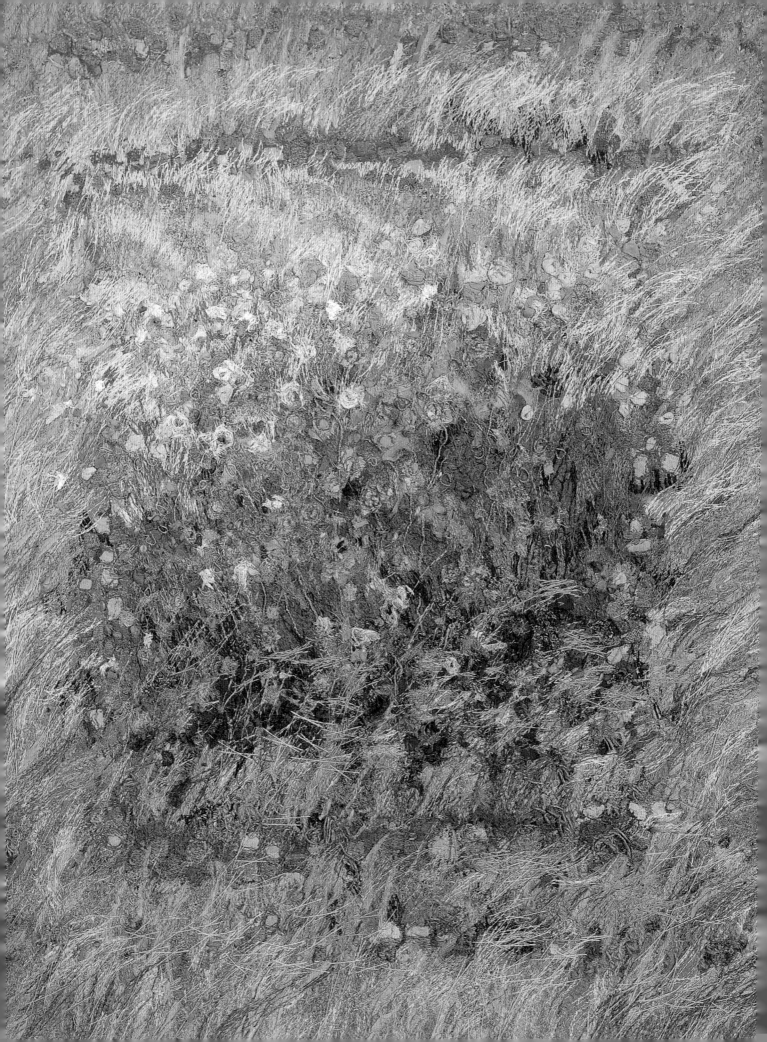

5

Combining Hand and Machine Stitching

There are many ways to create wonderful machine embroideries and many more textile artists now appreciate that machine and hand stitches can make an exciting partnership. This is because the finer tracery of the machine stitch contrasts well with, and complements, the bolder textured mark made by hand stitches. It is customary to create the pattern or picture by machine stitching the imagery in the first place and then adding a few appropriate hand stitches to mingle into and encrust the surface, the shadows created by the higher relief offering an interesting textural effect.

Hand into Machine Stitching

Some textile artists machine stitch the ground fabric in order to block in and layer subtle changes of colour and tone to create strong images before embarking on the surface hand stitches to highlight certain prime aspects, the scale of stitch and quality of yarn playing a decisive role. However, unusual and surprising results can be achieved by hand stitching the fabric first followed by machine stitching to flatten certain parts and allowing others to stand proud. The ridges and indentations created offer sculptured surfaces which can be most attractive (see pages 94–5 for further explanations and inspiration).

The most recent and innovative development is a method of making a machine lace by stitching onto soluble cloth. This can be achieved by stitching a design on the cloth, ensuring that all sections are linked. Closely worked areas of decorative stitching can contrast with delicate edges and other additions. When this unique surface is dissolved in water, a new 'lacy' cloth is revealed. The joy is that this technique allows the worker complete control over the colour, texture and pattern of the new fabric. Another appealing quality is the fact that the edges do not fray.

There are several soluble fabrics on the market, and each has their own characteristics. The cold water-soluble film looks and feels like a thin plastic. It is useful as a stabiliser to support a flimsy material, but would not be able to withstand the weight of densely worked stitchery without splitting. The thicker type, called 'Aquafilm', and especially the boiling water-soluble variety which looks like an organdy fabric, is much more suitable for creating heavier textural surfaces or intricate edgings. These materials give almost unlimited creative potential to combining machine and hand stitches.

Detail from 'Where Serpents Sleep', Crete Series. The background cloth was made by machine stitching onto soluble fabric. Long straight stitches were hand stitched on the fabric, before additional machine stitching was worked into them. Free cross stitches, detached chain, straight stitches and knots further embellish the surface. **Jan Beaney**

Exciting and unexpected results can be achieved by first machine stitching a grid on to soluble fabric in order to support the hand stitches to be worked on top. On completion the ground cloth is dissolved, leaving the chunkier, textured hand stitches contrasting with the lacy openwork.

Before starting, spend some time doodling on paper to determine the general structure of the chosen stitch so that a linking or supporting base of machine stitches can be planned. You will need to decide where the stitch will be fastened on and off as well as the position of the needle placements during the formation of the stitch. The general aim is to create a machine-stitched surface to hand stitch into but it will not necessarily feature when the soluble fabric is dissolved away. If chunkier areas of stitching are required wider bands of machining will need to be made.

First of all draw the main guidelines on the cloth and thread the machine with a colour that will blend with your chosen colour scheme. The machine can be set for normal stitching if straight line networks are appropriate. However, if curvy or more intricate shapes are required it should be set for free hand machining. Stitches should be cross-hatched to form a mesh, in order to give a firm base to support the handwork to be stitched on top. A finer effect can be achieved by a network consisting of at least two lines machined on top of each other, to supply the tracery into which to darn, loop or chain stitch the threads. Experiment with embellishing the network with thick or thin yarns, as these will give different results.

Remember

- to ensure that all machine lines are linked throughout. If this first stage is not constructed properly the piece will fall apart during the dissolving process.
- to carefully pin out the completed stitchery on a piece of polystyrene (styrofoam), so that it keeps its shape during the dissolving process.
- to be aware that if home dyed yarns are included they may loose some colour when immersed in hot or boiling water. However, threads can always be re-coloured.
- that the boiling water-soluble fabric is more pleasurable one to stitch into, but can have the disadvantages mentioned. Commercially dyed yarns seem not to be affected.
- to consider embroidering the pattern in white or cream threads and to colour them after the material has been dissolved.

Other exciting openwork fabric can be made by knotting, looping, lashing together hand- or machine-made cords into a symmetrical or asymmetrical arrangement. Supporting this structure on water-soluble fabric will help enable this process to be carried out more easily. Having created a pattern, you may like to consider the possibility of hand stitching over and through the cords and across the open spaces. Many stitches need just a line or bar of thread initially to support them. Raised chain band, lock stitch, buttonhole variations and darning are some to consider. Mixed media, beads or fabric strips incorporated could give alternative effects.

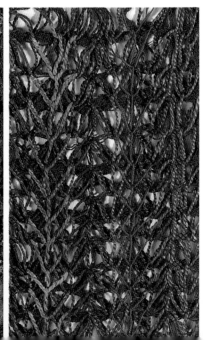

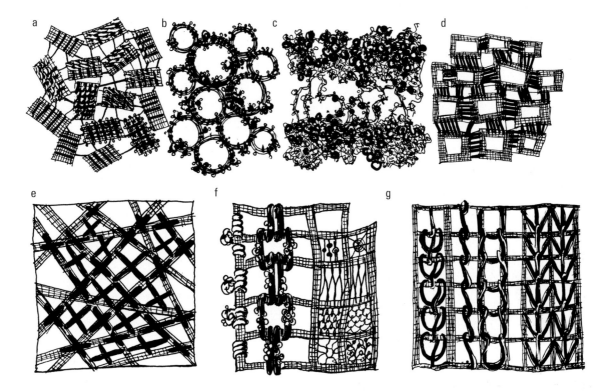

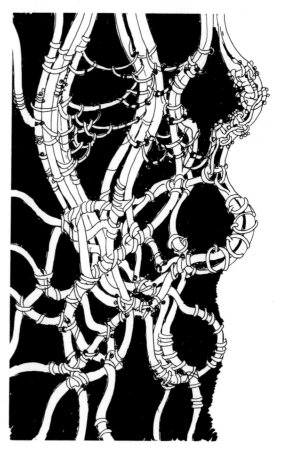

(Above) This first sketch shows ideas for making machine stitched grids on soluble fabric, in order to support hand stitching. The machined lines should be connected to form a mesh, so that the machined and hand-stitched lace will not fall apart when the soluble fabric is dissolved.

a   Machined grid plus stern stitch worked over straight stitch bars
b   Interconnected machined lines wrapped with embroidery threads and beads
c   A scribbly machined mesh to support groups of various sized French knots
d   Frames of machined grids all connected to each other, before working groups of straight stitches
e   Haphazard machined bars to support cross stitches as well as provide a structure for the stitches to be worked across the space
f   A grid showing lock stitch, wrapping, cretan and buttonhole filling stitches
g   Raised chain band, stern, open chain and fly stitches worked over a finer machined network.

(Right) This sketch shows a number of ways that hand or machine-wrapped cords could be darned, lashed or knotted together to form an interesting network. This could then be applied to a conventional backcloth, after which other stitches could be worked on top or across the structure. Alternatively, the cords could be supported on soluble fabric, in order to provide an easier method for creating the arrangement before the additional stitching is worked. On completion, the soluble fabric can be dissolved in water to leave a textured, lacy openwork pattern. **Jan Beaney**

(Facing page) Raised chain band (far left), lock stitch (middle left) and fly stitch (left) worked into a machine-stitched grid on soluble fabrics. **Jan Beaney**

Machine into Hand Stitching

Machine and hand stitch are often combined to good effect. The most obvious method is to hand stitch over a machine surface. An alternative approach is to hand stitch first and then machine over and into it. This is an effective strategy for making bolder marks with machine embroidery.

Machine stitching makes a fine mark and is capable of the most exquisite tracery and textures, but there is a limit to the size of the thread which can be used. Bolder marks are possible using the widest zig zag, but even then bolder marks are often required, particularly on larger scale pieces. The secret of successful working into hand stitching is to adopt a bold approach. Small, subtle stitches could be overpowered, so it is best to use a thick thread and strong, rhythmic movements.

The tone of the threads will also need to be carefully considered. When starting, machine and hand stitching in similar tones will build up confidence in this technique.

When machining over heavy textures with free machine embroidery, stabilize the background as well as you can, and use a frame or support the fabric. A darning foot will help to keep the textures manageable. When dealing with highly textured areas, work very slowly at first to avoid breaking needles.

The success of this technique depends on sensitivity to the rhythms and shapes of the hand stitching and not swamping it. Echo the patterning and work the stitches, allowing raised textures to emerge through the machining. It is possible to make highly textured cloths in this way and you can extend the range of marks for machine stitching for large-scale textiles.

(Facing page) The ground fabric for this stitched texture consists of a very loosely knitted structure, couched down and then stitched with knotted cable chain. The machine stitching had to be worked carefully because of the rough texture and supported in a frame with the surface as taut as possible. This sample has been left incomplete to reveal the staged processes.
Jean Littlejohn

Free appliqué with hand stitch was worked before the machine stitching to create a highly decorative but functional surface for this bag. **Angela Elliot**

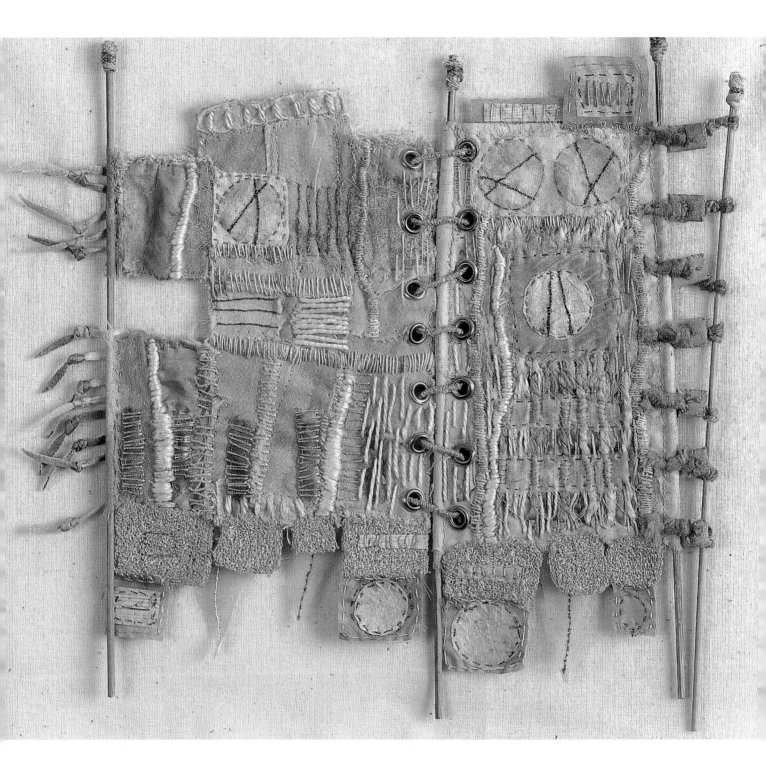

This mixed media piece celebrates the creative use of joinings. A range of techniques have been used including lacing and overcasting.

Jen Chamberlain

6

Using Stitches

Stitches can be used for specific purposes. Focusing on some of the principal ways of applying stitches – for joinings, borders, edges, grids, marks, landscapes and texture – this section illustrates how to structure your approach to each one.

Stitches as Joinings

There are times when you need to join pieces of fabric together – either touching or not touching. Recycled materials feature strongly in many contemporary textiles and these often require functional joinings. Since fabric shortage is rarely a problem, the joinings required usually have a relationship to the nature of the image or are used as a decorative feature. By exploring the different methods of joining pieces of fabric together, you can add vigour and energy to enliven your embroideries. With a variety of methods at your disposal, it is possible to use this element to add to the thrust of the work.

Insertion stitches or decorative open seams have long been used as a method of joining two non-touching edges together. There is a formality to the technique because it is most often used for household or fashion items. A useful exercise to encourage a more inventive approach to joinings is to take some pieces of fabric and join them together in as many ways as possible without the use of a needle and thread. This is not as difficult as it might at first appear and certainly echoes the challenge that confronted early man who needed to join animal skins to keep warm. Over the centuries these early lacings and tyings, wrappings and toggles developed into highly sophisticated polished techniques.

This exercise will give you a fresh approach to utilising joinings.

As with all techniques you need to consider the overall look and not overpower the embroidery with the joinings unless they are the main feature. Select simple forms where the joinings are there as spacers or as a device to display the main elements of the embroidery. However there are times when you can celebrate the nature of these stitches and use them with a flourish. An example might be a textured wall, where the stone pieces forming the wall are the main feature. When joining them together with open seams, make sure that they reflect the feeling of the natural stone. Fussy and intricate stitches would just draw attention to the gaps and detract from the image. In a more ornate piece, the joinings can reflect this quality and add decorative elements to the work.

On a technical note, when working both traditional or non-traditional insertion stitches they need to be supported on a piece of stiff paper or something similar. Tack the two pieces to be joined together on the paper with the required space between them and work the subsequent stitches without stitching into the paper. When complete, remove the tacking stitches to reveal the whole fabric.

(Next spread) Cloth for the Lycian Kings, worked on an old beach wrap faded by years of Turkish sun. The act of hand stitching one cloth to another defines the form of this embroiderer's work. Mostly running or darning stitches are used as a fluent way of joining textile fragments. Reflecting a momentary mood or 'tension', stitch becomes a physical link between the real and imagined world of myth and symbol. **Julia Caprara**

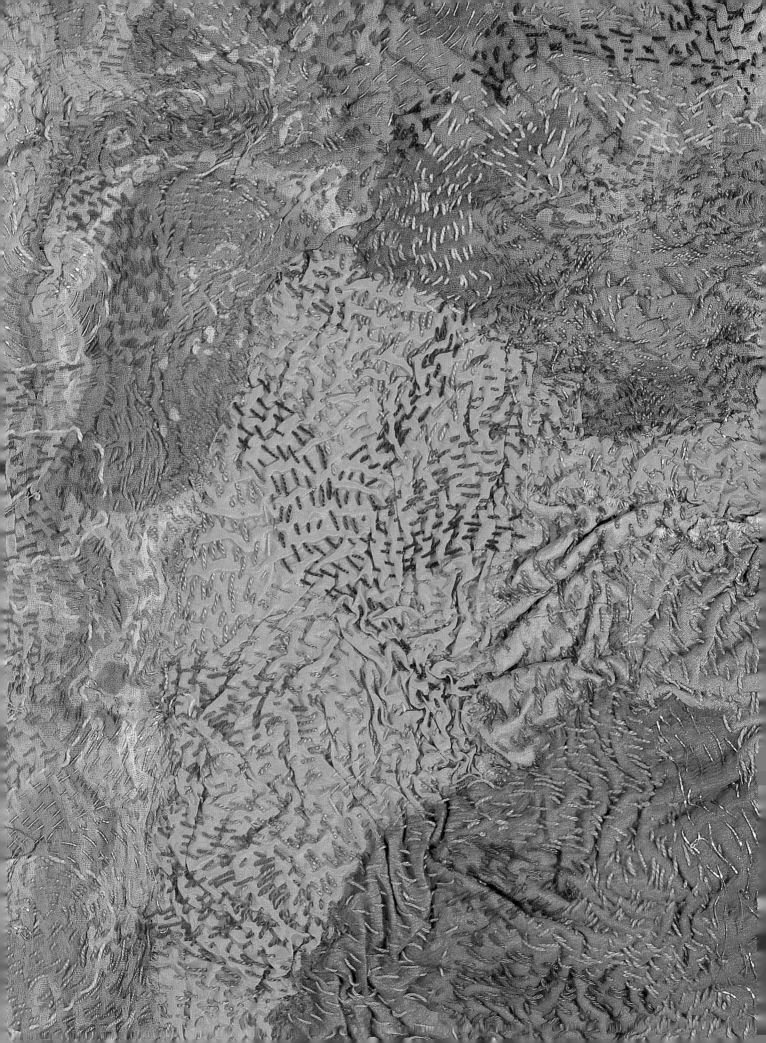

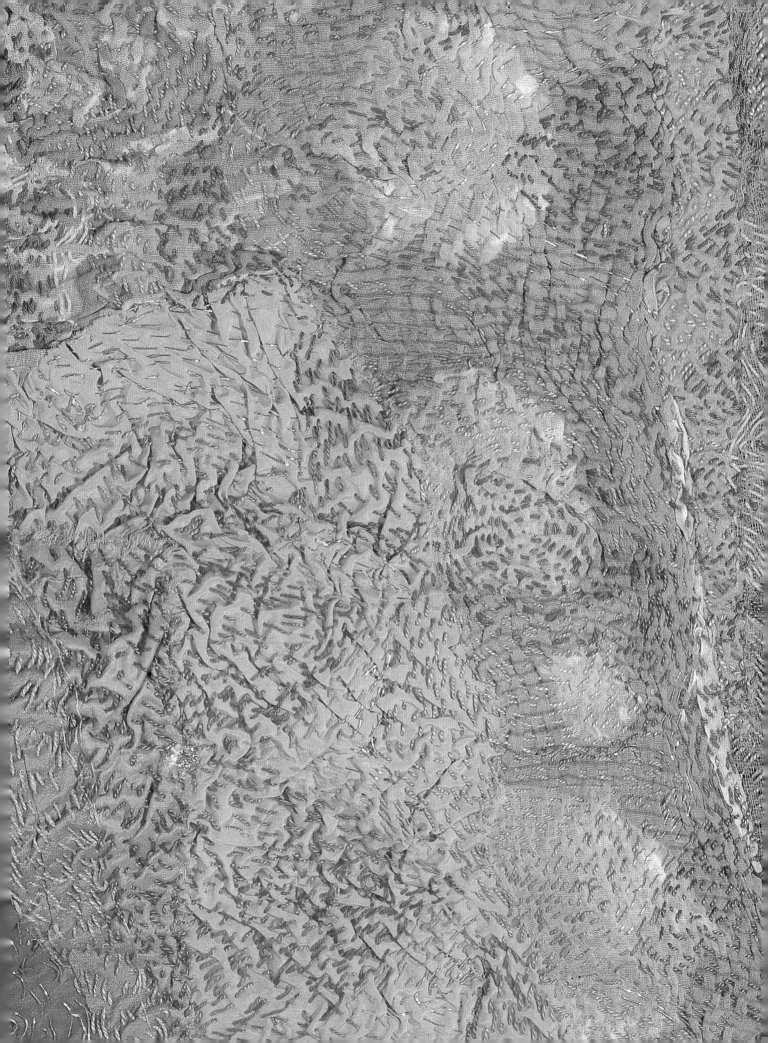

Stitches as Borders

Designing a decorative border for a piece of work is always challenging and can be most rewarding if the partnership between it and the background is compatible. If it is the main focus of a garment, a fashion accessory or a household item, the design for the embroidery should be colour co-ordinated and planned to look comfortable on the ground fabric. Textural or patterned aspects of the main cloth should be reflected in the border embroidery in order to link and integrate the elements.

There is a wealth of intriguing shapes around you in everyday life which could inspire simple or complex border patterns. Symmetrical ones may be developed from wood carvings, ironwork, tiles, coal holes, ethnic jewellery or plant structures. Simplified arrangements of shapes influenced by lichen, mosses, animal markings, rust and tree bark can be repeated haphazardly to make a balanced, asymmetrical border.

Scale is always an aspect to be considered. By changing the size of the shapes, stitches and threads within the pattern, a more satisfying combination will emerge. For contrast, combine wide stripes with narrow ridges, small and large motifs, fine and chunky threads and matt and shiny yarns, which will prevent the border from becoming visually boring and give it more dynamism.

The 'highs' and 'lows' of a stitch arrangement add another dimension as the cast shadows create further interest. Imagine a cross section of an ornately carved or moulded picture frame. The ridges and indentations vary in depth and width, and the surfaces can be smooth, embossed or have intricate protrusions. If some of these characteristics are interpreted by layering, decorating and contrasting the scale of the stitch patterns, the resulting borders could be really exciting.

These painted designs were inspired by sketches of stone carving on a Chinatown gateway, a carved and gilded doorway in a Paris museum and decorative stonework from Chartres Cathedral. The edging embroidery shows knotted wool and cotton, knitting tape, paper string, felt and muslin strips, all couched down with perlé, metallic and faceted yarns. Seeding stitches link the bands of circular shapes. **Jan Beaney**

There are many occasions when a stitched border is needed, either as an edging to a functional item or for framing a composition. The border should always reflect the fabric and momentum of the rest of the stitched textile. Be careful not to allow a border to dominate and overwhelm a composition.

A wealth of inspiration can be gained by looking at embroideries from other cultures. Most countries have borders in their stitched textiles because they fit so well into the basic shapes of the traditional costume. In some countries, such as Hungary, the costume and domestic embroideries feature lavish borders which take over the whole fabric. Similarly in parts of India where hand stitch is widely practised, borders are a strong element in the designs. Borders such as these involve elaborate variations on a theme with one or two main features and many 'filling in' stitches which take off in imaginative flights of fancy. The basic motifs are long established, traditional and symbolic patterns which become more and more decorative and innovative as they are reworked through the generations.

Complex looking patterns often have an underpinning simplicity and time is well spent in finding the basis of the pattern if you want to create your own. They are frequently based on the structure of the fabric and follow a vertical, horizontal or diagonal format. Where the structure is less defined, there is usually a main group of shapes around which the variations are developed. This can be likened to a musical composition, where the central theme diminishes and rises. Against this structure other musical themes are introduced and thematic echoes recur throughout. The main theme dictates the whole structure, but still allows for variations.

Other aspects which you can use apart from the actual pattern could include the colours, proportions and the stitches. Sometimes stitches will be hard to identify without a magnifying glass but this can be a worthwhile exercise. Also remember that where a colour runs out, a line might well be finished in a different hue although the general pattern qualities are still maintained. This can be helpful when trying not to be too rigid. Cut paper is another excellent way of creating your own pattern inspiration, particularly when a fairly complex border is required.

(Facing page) This stitched textile from India contains borders of colourful stitches which could provide endless inspiration for stitch ideas.

*(Below) This freely worked piece, inspired by the textile opposite, is worked in borders using interlaced herringbone stitch as the framework, with whipping, French knots and knotted cable chain for highlights. **Jean Littlejohn***

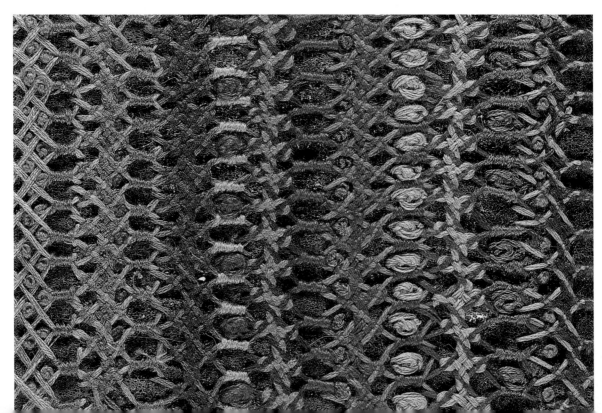

Stitches as Edges

In the past, a limited selection of stitches has been used to decorate edgings on garments and household linen. In most instances the priority has been to choose a stitch that will do the job of holding the fabric turning in place in a decorative manner, but without featuring prominently. On many items these predictable stitches are entirely appropriate for the purpose; they are charming and should not be derided. They can, however, be reconsidered by working with the wealth of wondrous threads and yarns now available.

For a new approach, challenge yourself by considering a range of other stitches not normally used to edge a cloth and that are certainly not listed as such in conventional stitch books. Initially renew your acquaintance with your chosen stitch and experiment working it as a line stitch, a single unit, in layers, horizontally and vertically. By stitching a number of trials and adjusting the size, spacing and tension, unexpected and delightful edges could result.

Some stitches such as buttonhole variations or pendant couching can be placed close to the edge to protrude attractively, whilst others may benefit from further techniques. For instance, raised chain band or cross stitches can be embroidered as separate units and the part of the stitch nearest the edge of the cloth can be emphasized by beading or wrapping in another thread in order to create decorative or encrusted nodules. Alternatively, other stitches such as raised stem band or open chain may have parts that can be adorned by darning, wrapping or suspending other threads, beads or mixed media. The extra weight will distort the stitch and allow it to overlap the edge in an attractive manner, thus holding the hem in place in a unique way.

Traditionally borders and edges tend to be symmetrical in treatment. Whichever arrangement of edging stitches you choose, endeavour to make the central area of work and the edges compatible and integrated. If the main embroidery is asymmetrical, the choice of stitch and its arrangement need to reflect these characteristics and be more casually placed, albeit balanced as a whole. The spacing and adornment can show a rhythmic repeating process without being too formal.

Remember

- to reflect aspects of the colour, textural quality and elements of the central stitched area in your choice of edging to create a good partnership (see stitch diagram, page 133).
- to tack your turning in place before the decorative stitching commences.
- to support your work on cold water-soluble film to enable you to set it in a frame if that is your preference. Some stitches are much easier to work if the fabric edge is tautly stretched.
- that some edging stitches can be richly or subtly adorned to feature as a border in their own right.
- to allow time to 'play' and experiment in order to develop this use of stitch.
- to be aware of other types of edges; interesting variations can be seen on embroideries from other parts of the world and could be inspirational.

(Above right) Couched threads, knots, buttonhole and fly stitch decorate this sample. A delicate fabric strip is threaded through a single fly stitch which edges the piece. **Amanda Martin**

(Above left) This sample is stitched with lines of raised chain band which have been layered in a grid arrangement. Beads have been incorporated in the top section. Single stitches form the edge and these too have been adorned with beads to form protruding nodules. **Jan Beaney**

(Right) This chunky design is worked in bands of different sizes of raised stem band stitch, resulting in a bold pattern. The outer stitch is wrapped and beaded, the weight of which distorts to achieve an attractive edging. **Jan Beaney**

Stitches as Grids

Grids imply a format and therefore act as a framework for those who wish to have a sense of security. Having said that, grids can be wonderfully imaginative stepping-stones for creating stitched textures without the restraints that an interpretive piece might hold. In such an example, the nature and quality of the stitches need to reflect the mood and atmosphere of the subject matter. If the grid is based on a natural form, such as a hedgerow, then the appropriate stitches need to be considered in the context of the design. It can be liberating to construct a grid based on simple geometric shapes and fill it with stitched 'flights of fancy'.

Grid formations are everywhere, so keep notes of patterns drawn from scaffolding, garden trellis, paving, machines, architecture and the numerous other sources. Develop them into grids which may be stitched, couched down in a flat pattern or built up dimensionally either with stitch or with added elements, such as beads, wrappings or knots.

(Facing page) The Shoowa cloth illustrated here is an African woven cloth made from beaten palm and worked with a raised stitch often described as Masai velvet. It contains simple rhythms that reflect patterns from a tribal culture celebrating symbolic elements formed into an infinite variety of grids. This cloth could inspire a range of grid formations integrated with your chosen colours and symbols.

(Below) Grid combining twigs and stitches. **Fiona Fletcher**

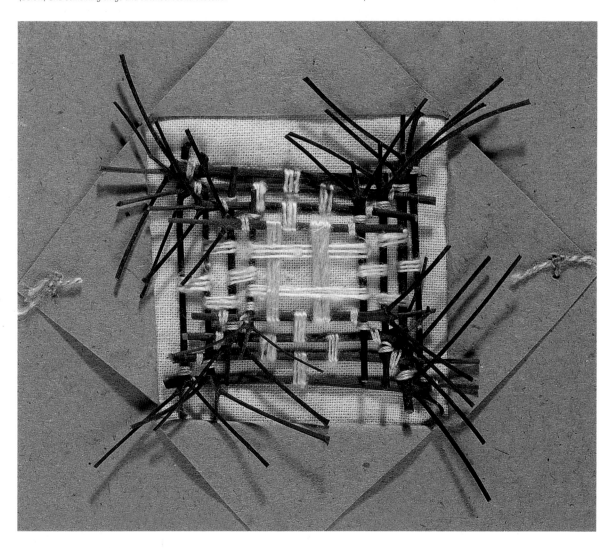

Using a simple grid from a Byzantine mosaic pattern as a framework, this 'free fall' grid has been worked in vibrant threads with couching and straight stitches in various thicknesses. These have been whipped in contrasting colours to highlight the rhythms within. **Jean Littlejohn**

Stitches as Marks

A stitch amounts to an expressive mark using thread on fabric – even the simple use of running stitch can alter the surface of cloth dramatically. Because of this, the placing of the stitch and the colour and thickness of the thread is crucial. Simplicity is often more difficult to achieve than rich texture. Where stitches are piled up and used in complex textures, the odd misplaced stitch could be introduced to give further exuberance to the surface. It is more difficult to place simple stitches boldly within a composition and it is an interesting exercise to bear this in mind when viewing the work of other embroiderers.

Knowing where to stop is difficult but with practice this becomes easier and it can be satisfying to achieve the effects you want by using a restrained approach. Train your eye to appreciate basic forms and compositions by looking at paintings, drawings and ceramics displaying an economy of line and mark..

Some of the simplest marks are the most effective. Seeing the zigzagged line in imagery from the past conjures up visions of early man using a stick to work this classic mark in the earth or sand. Crosses, lines and dots have the same quality.

Fly stitch on a ground of bubble wrap, melted and fused with fibres by ironing between pieces of baking parchment. **Jean Littlejohn**

Layers of medium quality pelmet Vilene were cut and bonded to form the
background of this piece. Straight stitches were worked before painting with
darkly coloured acrylic wax to give a really embedded feel. Using stitch in this
way gives a subtle and totally integrated look. Further surface stitches were
worked as a gentle contrast. **Jean Littlejohn**

Stitching a Landscape

Landscapes have always held a deep fascination for many artists working in a range of media. A poppy field, a bluebell wood, swaying clumps of rose bay willow herb- or thrift-covered cliffs may impress and trigger a number of emotional responses which can then be captured in stitch. These subjects have inspired many works, but often in a predictable way, so there is always scope for new interpretations.

Select a photograph of a landscape, preferably one you have taken yourself. List in order of preference why you liked, selected or photographed it. This exercise will help determine which aspects you wish to exaggerate or emphasize. Now list the main colours and the proportions. Isolate the main patterns, textures and marks out of context and make quick diagrams of each of them in turn. Are the marks placed diagonally or haphazardly, are they short and abrupt, graceful and flowing or criss-crossed and layered? Perhaps the general shapes are linear or geometric or made up of dots, blobs, blips and blocks. Working through these exercises will help you to look more intently and develop a personal involvement in your chosen landscape.

The next stage is to select from the picture a section or strip out of context to define the composition of shapes and the boundary. Sketch the main shapes very simply but note carefully the darker-toned shapes that run through the piece. This research

Inspired by a field of Linseed flowers, this sample uses grey green thread couched down with blue and olive green stranded cotton, capturing a watery look. Decorated couching, cross stitches and knots worked in a variety of thick and thin yarns form the border in which the miniature landscape is placed.
Jan Beaney

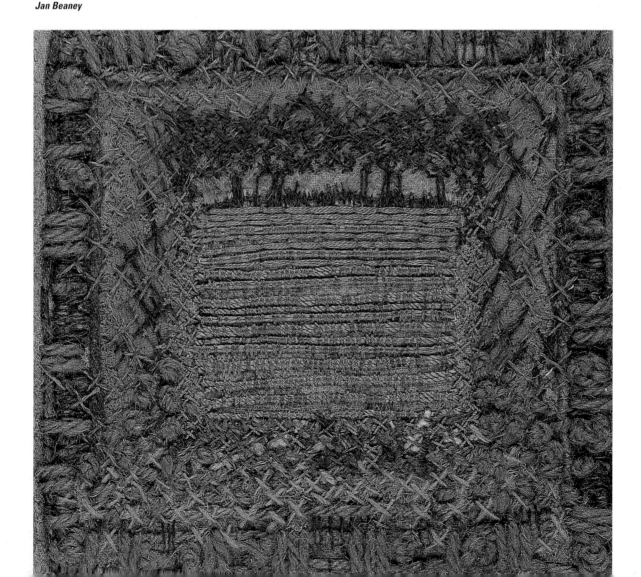

will enable you to depict this with dye, fabric or stitch and provide a linking mechanism at the outset. If the sketch or photograph is enlarged to the desired size of the intended embroidery, the dark, light and colour drifts can be traced through (see page 87) and will help the initial build-up of colour and tone.

Armed with this information, make a number of quick sketch diagrams, varying the positions of the main shapes, emphasizing or understating certain aspects. These can be varied in scale, pieced and patched, striped horizontally, vertically or diagonally, or placed within borders. Representative landscape images may be set within a decorative edging which should contain and reflect elements of the colour or textural qualities in the main

section. Alternatively abstract landscape images may be inspired by just the patterns or the colour scheme from your initial reference material.

Proceed with the embroidery by drawing or tacking the basic design lines on the backing cloth. You may prefer to dye, apply fabrics or create other textural backgrounds before marking out the important aspects. Having decided on the area of interest, block in the main stitches, developing and linking them throughout the whole piece before looking at highlighting, detailing and refining.

Fabric strips and iridescent plastic lacing couched to represent water. A variety of wool is stitched to suggest plant forms in the foreground.
Jan Beaney

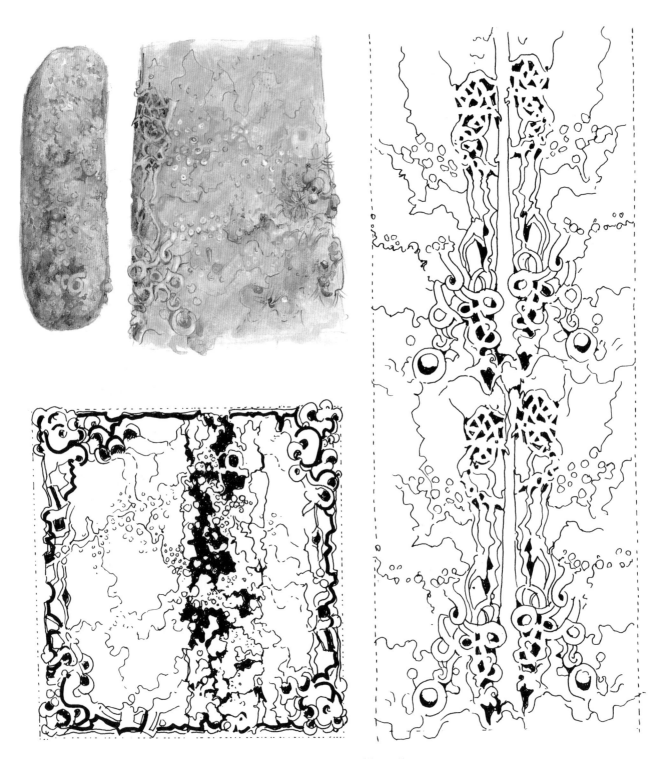

(Above left) A coloured sketch in aquarelle crayons of a delicately coloured encrusted stone. The left-hand side of the larger colour piece was selected for a linear pattern which was repeated as a slightly offset mirror image, as well as lengthways to form a border (above right). A similar section of the original drawing was used to make the square format design (below left), whereas the strip highlighted within the shape was inspired by the smaller stone – this could also be a textured, striped pattern in its own right. **Jan Beaney**

Textural Inspiration

Embroiderers are always fascinated by textural surfaces because of their tactile qualities and their compatibililty to fabric and threads. Gathering information on a theme is crucial and here are included some tips on moving from the initial observation to developing inspirational material.

For example, when beach combing, people love to find stones with pretty colours and attractive markings or shells that glimmer or have encrusted surfaces. Crab shells, rock surfaces, seaweed, sand and water patterns can be just as inspirational. A walk in the wood offers a different situation, where you can respond to the variety of colour, texture and patterns to be found in lichen, mosses, tree bark, fungi or birds' feathers. Rust, rotted wood, old walls, rockeries and even mildew are other surfaces that offer superb colour and textural inspiration.

Collect information by describing the surfaces in words and making a sketch or taking a photograph. This reference will help you develop a colour scheme, fabric and threads. Deciding which patterns or textures to convert into a suitable stitched piece is often the main challenge. This process can be made easier by isolating your observations. Initially select the areas of a surface that appeal the most, listing your reasons. Consider the colours and their proportions and then describe the textural qualities in order to determine the characteristics of the marks you wish to emphasize. The following list of words conjures up a number of textural marks and arrangements:

blips	**dots**	**speckles**
blobs	**flowing**	**splatters**
blocks	**frilly**	**splodges**
bumps	**fuzzy**	**spots**
craggy	**jagged**	**squiggles**
criss-crossed	**meandering**	**undulating**
dashes	**ridged**	**wavy**

Seeding and French knots are obvious choices as responses to this collection of words, but other stitches worked as a single unit may be more suitable. Rosette and twisted chain stitches could be blips or splodges or detached chain might be layered to form bumps or blocks. Describing the textural placements of a surface may clarify its quality, inspiring you to encroach, group, layer or crosshatch these stitches to represent your chosen surface. Noting other features, such as whether the background is shiny, spongy, flaky, crumbly, velvety or encrusted, will help determine the preparation for the ground fabric.

Using a photocopier, enlarge your rough diagrams, sketches or photographs so it is easy to draw or trace the areas you wish to use. Photocopy these drawings or tracings several times, changing the scale to experiment with a variety of placements. Arrange some of the shapes as repeating patterns, back to back, striped or in blocks. If selecting a border pattern, the central area may need to include other aspects from the original design source. The design can be contrived if necessary by using additional lines or drifts of colour to link the parts. Select a focal point – perhaps an area of high texture or highlighted colour.

As well as inspiring an element of a representational image, these ideas could be used for textural decoration, such as strips of pattern to embellish a belt, a hat band, or an edging on a garment. Square or rectangular designs could be made into box tops, pretty bags or on a smaller scale as brooches and pendants.

The intriguing lumpy texture of this section of burnt wood (above) inspired the stitched sample (facing page). Many layers of raised stem band stitches form the high relief. These surfaces have been decorated with a range of gimps, sparkling crochet yarn, chenille, nylon tape and beads exaggerating the shine and reflections shown in the photograph. *Jan Beaney*

A collection of holiday sketches with aquarelle crayons, water and gouache which could inspire colour ideas as well as textural patterns.

(Above left) A section of stone, (Above right) Two views of an encrusted shell (Below left) A glimpse through water at two types of seaweed attached to the rocks, (Below right) A section of a knobbly, textured shell, inspiring the sample opposite. The pink colour was far more pronounced when wet and the colour faded quite quickly, which was a little confusing during the painting process.

(Facing page) This experimental piece was inspired by the highly textured surfaces shown above. To colour and stiffen, scrim was painted with metallic fabric paints and metallic powders were mixed with a fabric medium and texture gel. Once dried and fixed with an iron, strips of the knotted fabric were couched in place onto a fabric painted ground cloth. Smaller knotted strips and straight stitches worked on the knots provide contrasting marks as well as helping to link and integrate the whole piece. **Jan Beaney**

7

Gallery

From the many featured approaches to handstitching surfaces in this book, it is hoped that you will have found a style to suit your method of working. For this chapter, we have approached embroiderers whose work exploits stitched texture and markmaking with exuberance and flair. The gallery of contemporary embroideries which follows offers inspiration to us all – covering a range of different approaches and in their own individual way, each embroiderer celebrates the versatility and the magic of the stitch.

(Facing page) A joyous pieced background on vibrantly coloured fabrics sets the tone for a liberated, simple approach to stitch marks. **Alison Goode**

(Next spread) Using a tablecloth with a lace border as the starting point, rules were set for the structure of this piece from which a detail is shown. It was decided that the patterned rug would be shown in a flat, vertical plane, with the bowl of fruit presented as three-dimmensional. By using many layers of very simple stitches with varying thicknesses of threads, this interpretation evolved from three commonplace objects – a bowl, apples, pears and oranges. **Audrey Walker**

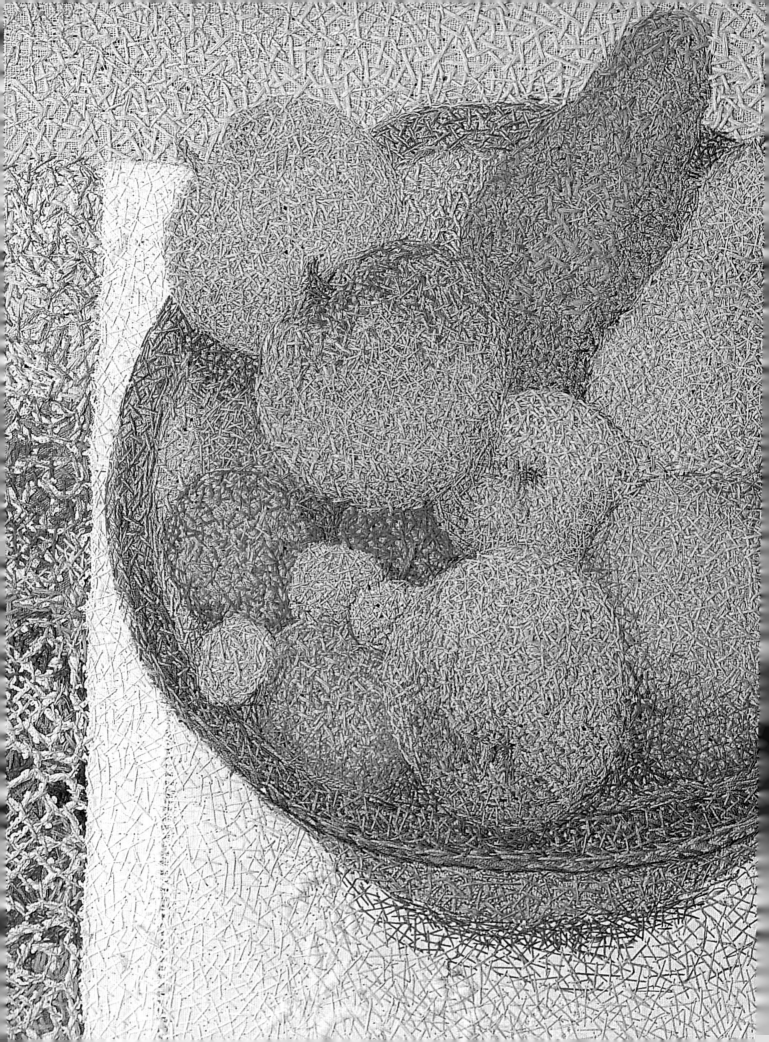

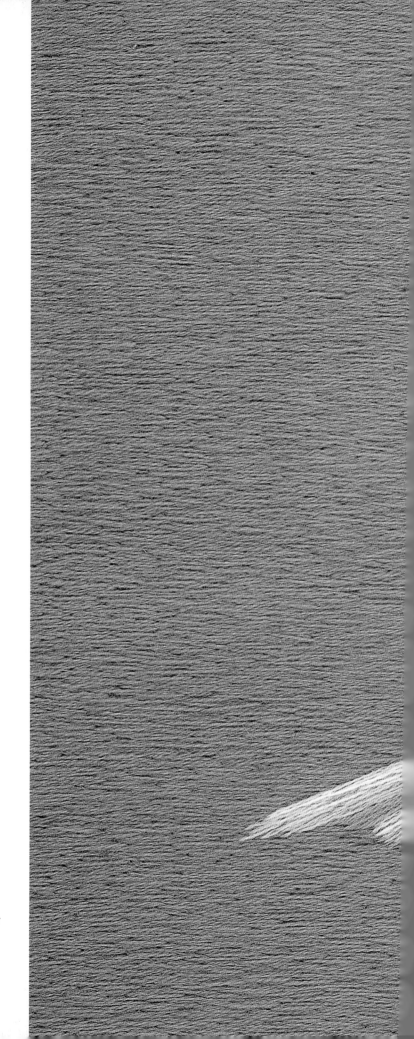

(Next spread) Feet in the Soil, an interpretation of the Arizona landscape. Repetitive hand stitching is used to restructure the fabric, creating surface rhythm and movement. **Jean Draper**

(Right) Flying into the Sun, a study of one of the doves living outside this embroiderer's studio, whose movements are a constant source of delight. Several layers of straight stitches completely cover the ground of Welsh flannel. The sensual pleasure of hand stitching in crewel wool on this fabric gives an added excitement. **Eirian Short**

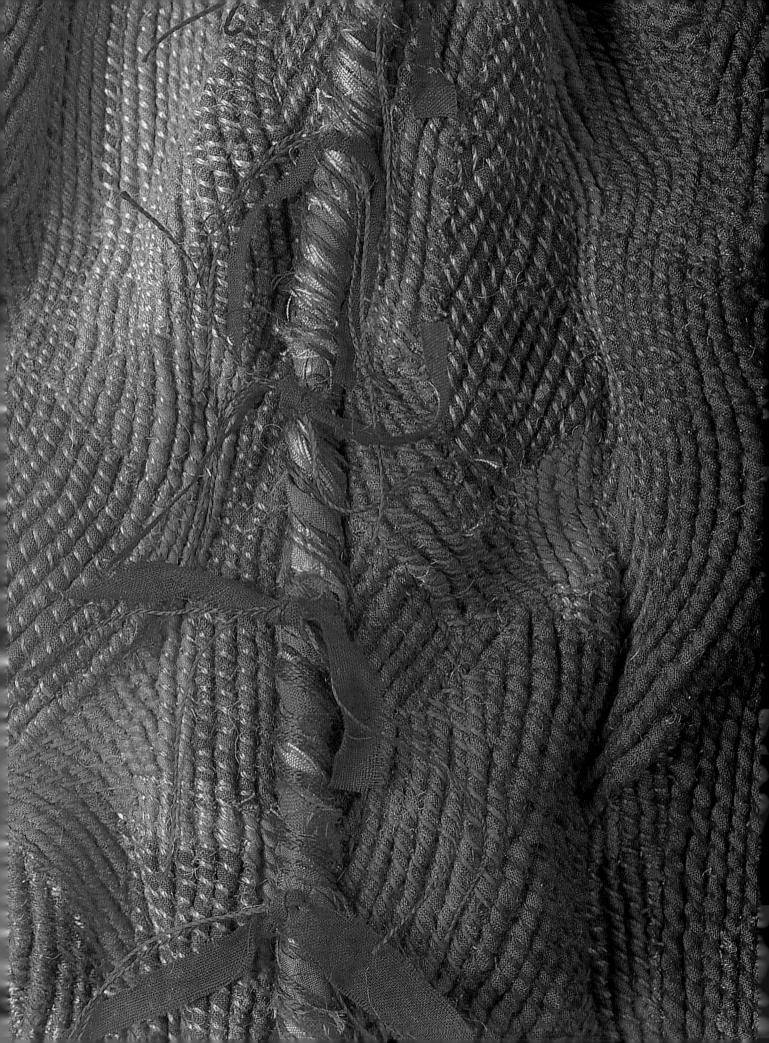

(Above) This exquisitely worked, tiny example of Or Nué depicts a simple still life. A deceptively understated image, it uses a labour intensive, traditional couching technique. **Barbara Antjoule**

(Facing page) Unearthed; Ukraine, a piece inspired by the surface qualities of an ancient pot in the British Museum. The ground fabric is a collage of torn strips and patches of painted cloth. Hand stitching, frequently on top of machine stitching, depicts the marks made by the ravages of time, and helps give a final emphasis to the layered, worn characteristics within the embroidery. **Gwen Hedley**

Conclusion

Stitchers should beware that, once started, stitching becomes compulsive. It can be rhythmic, tactile, sensuous and rewarding and when things go well there is always the satisfaction of knowing that you have created a stitched cloth with the simplest of tools and equipment.

There are so many stitches, and so little time, but we hope that by structuring your approach to developing new ways of stitching, the time you spend at your embroidery will be effective and pleasurable. Set yourself new challenges – try an unfamiliar stitch or revise its method and work it in a variety of ways. We have emphasized throughout that favourite stitches can so often be predictable and may not stretch your creative potential, so try to always think beyond them. There are really only a few basic stitch constructions, but so many endless variations. Look through a selection of traditional stitch books which may provide some obscure stitches as inspiration.

Embroiderers have always been challenged and excited by newly discovered materials and techniques and this is still the case today. New products for colouring or encrusting fabric and new methods for whipping, interlacing and building up stitches, used selectively will continually encourage embroiderers to cross boundaries and create magical stitched textiles. The fascination of embroidery is the actual process of stitching into a fabric and transforming its surface. However many stitch variations we might discover, ultimately we all work with a needle, yarn and a background fabric – this is our common heritage. In addition, this is the reason why we seek to share our own discoveries now – to enrich the embroideries of the future in the same way as those of the past have enriched ours of today.

Stitched piece inspired by rock formations. A photograph was printed by photo transfer paper on a copier machine onto a cotton cloth. The surfaces are coloured with metallic fabric paints, layers of cellophane and Tyvek, the latter stitched with running stitches and knots with the loops left to protrude. Romanian couching is used as a line stitch and as single units. **Jan Beaney**

Stitch Diagrams

There are many books illustrating conventional stitch diagrams which are very useful for reference. In this section you will find a series of stitch diagrams following a style devised to present stitch variations clearly to readers. These diagrams also enable the visualisation and development of your own stitch interpretations. The groupings have been selected to exploit themes and particular stitch attributes. These may prove a good starting point for your own creative stitch explorations.

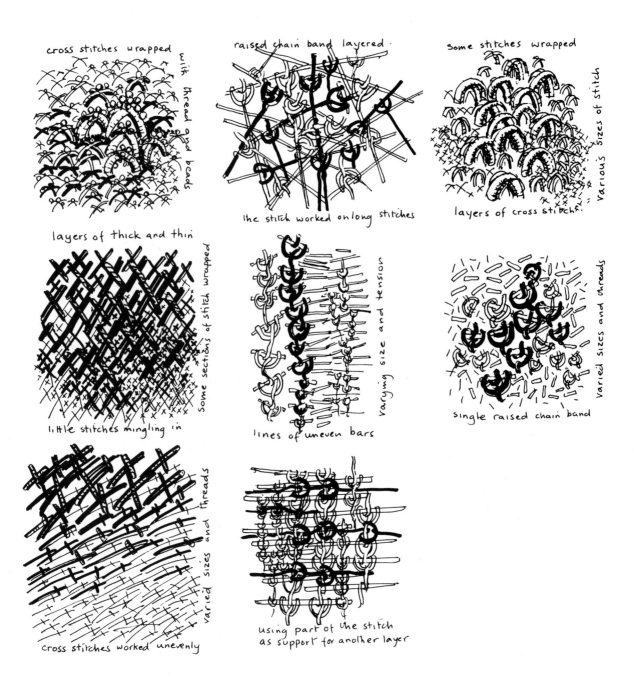

cross stitches wrapped with thread and beads

raised chain band layered.

the stitch worked on long stitches

some stitches wrapped

various sizes of stitch

layers of cross stitches.

layers of thick and thin

Some sections of stitch wrapped

little stitches mingling in

Varying size and tension

lines of uneven bars

Varied sizes and threads

single raised chain band

Varied sizes and threads

cross stitches worked unevenly

using part of the stitch as support for another layer

EDGES

single raised chain band

Partially wrapped cross stitches in centre panel

sections wrapped with beads

long legged french knots in central panel

single fly stitches with beads

Pendant couching in central area

Roumanian couching

beaded buttonhole in centre

lock stitch with outer section beaded.

OPEN CHAIN STITCH

open chain worked in lines

Variety of size and thread

single units set inside the chain

Single stitches to form crosses

thick   thin

single units of open chain

open chain worked as single units

open chain worked as

longer stitches than normal.

set inside another

knotted buttonhole filling anchored at the end of each row

detached buttonhole ring

knotted buttonhole filling loose at each row end distorts.

long laid threads wrapped into groups

needleweaving produces exciting nets and open structures

open buttonhole filling

overlapping detached buttonhole bars may be piled up in vigorous textures.

cork stitch worked regularly and irregularly

satin stitch eyelets

Feather stitch

Buttonhole in overlapping sweeps.....

irregular buttonhole

Stitches to create open and lace like structures

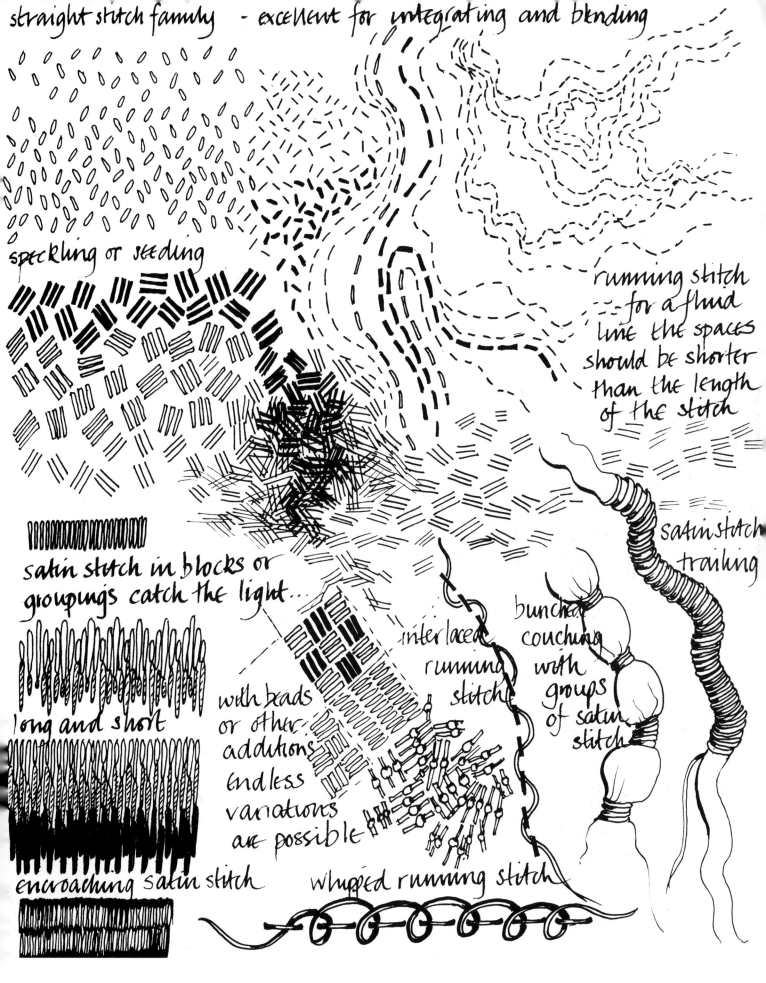

straight stitch family — excellent for integrating and blending

speckling or seeding

running stitch — for a fluid line the spaces should be shorter than the length of the stitch

satin stitch in blocks or groupings catch the light...

long and short

encroaching satin stitch

with beads or other additions endless variations are possible

interlaced running stitch

whipped running stitch

bunched couching with groups of satin stitch

satin stitch trailing

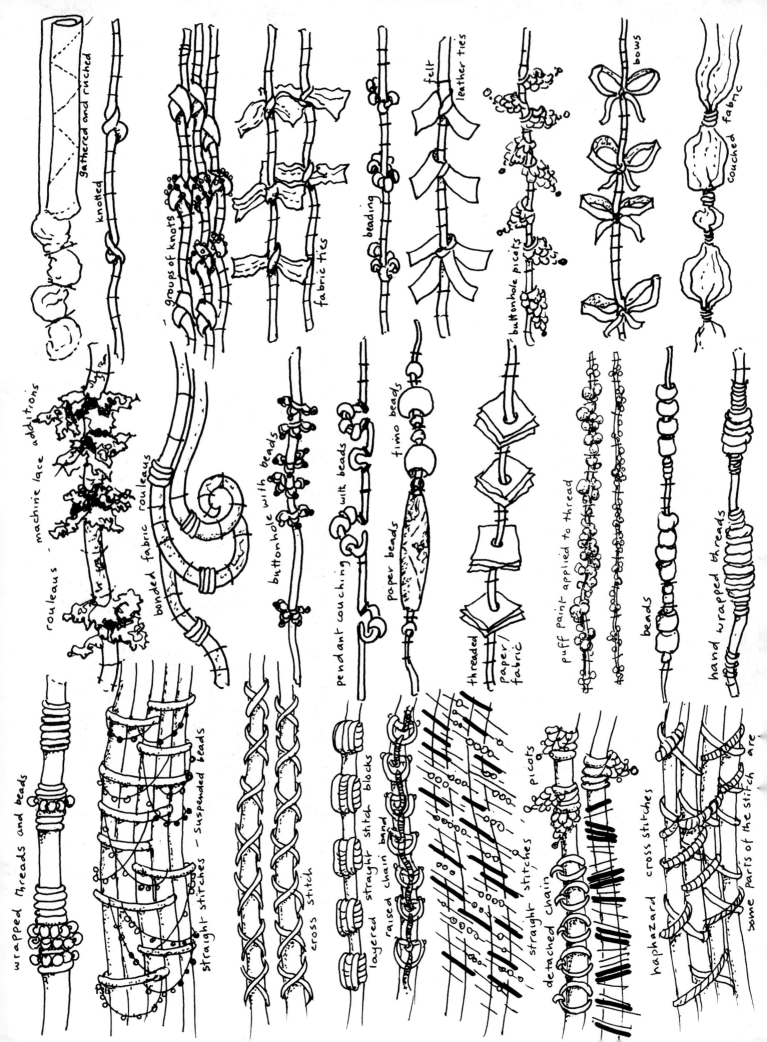

gathered and ruched

knotted

groups of knots

fabric ties

beading

felt

leather ties

buttonhole picots

bows

couched fabric

rouleaus - machine lace additions

bonded fabric rouleaus

buttonhole with beads

pendant couching with beads

paper beads

fimo beads

threaded paper / fabric

puff paint applied to thread

beads

hand wrapped threads

wrapped threads and beads

straight stitches - suspended beads

cross stitch

layered straight stitch blocks

raised chain band

straight stitches

detached chain

picots

haphazard cross stitches

some parts of the stitch are

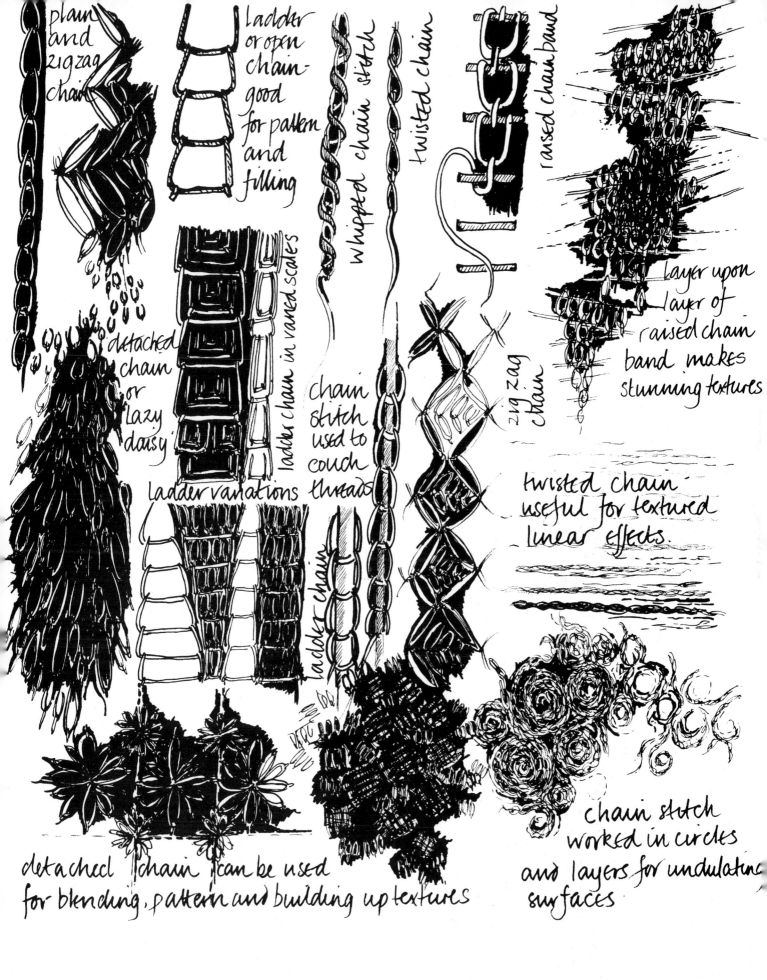

plain and zigzag chain

Ladder or open chain - good for pattern and filling

whipped chain stitch

twisted chain

raised chain band

detached chain or lazy daisy

ladder chain in varied scales

chain stitch used to couch threads

zig zag chain

Ladder variations

ladder chain

layer upon layer of raised chain band makes stunning textures

twisted chain useful for textured linear effects.

chain stitch worked in circles and layers for undulating surfaces

detached chain can be used for blending, pattern and building up textures

137

Glossary

Abstract Images using colour, form or texture, which do not necessarily represent recognisable objects.

Acrylic paint A quick-drying synthetic paint with a shiny appearance. Soluble in water, it can be used to create textured surfaces. Varying in thickness and composition, some types are designed for use on fabrics, watered down for a wash or mixed with a medium for printing, as they are for thicker textures.

Aquarelle Colouring media such as pencils or crayons which can be blended in water.

Asymmetry Two halves that are not balanced or equal about a central line (not mirror images of each other).

Baking parchment This non-stick (silicone) paper used for baking seems to be the only paper, apart from the one backing the bonding adhesive, which does not stick to the materials or iron when bonding applied shapes. It is also useful for protecting the iron when shrinking and distorting heat-sensitive materials such as Tyvek and cellophane.

Beading needle An extremely fine long needle for sewing on small beads.

Bonding paper or transfer fusing web Paper backed with a fine layer of adhesive. It is used for some types of intricate appliqué as it stiffens the fabric and makes it easier to cut out the shapes. It may be coloured with a range of liquid media such as acrylics or silk paints. The adhesive shrinks and ripples when wet and after drying it may be ironed on the fabric where the interesting patterns will enhance the surface. It retains its adhesive qualities and scraps and fibres may be added to the surface and ironed on with baking parchment over the top.

Buttonhole picots Work two small straight stitches bringing the thread out just above the left-hand end. Commence working buttonhole stitches over the bar only and not through the fabric. One line produces a ring picot. By turning the needle, and without going into the cloth, make a return journey, working buttonhole stitches into the last line of stitches. A number of rows can be worked in this manner resulting in long pieces of stitching which can be manipulated into unusual textural surfaces. Triangular or pointed picots can be made by decreasing one stitch on each journey. To finish off, darn the thread up one side of the picot and fasten off at the back near the original straight stitches.

Card window A rectangular or square shape cut from a piece of card which can be placed over a design source to identify and select areas of interest. It is very useful as it cuts out the distracting peripheral detail.

Chenille needle A sharp, pointed needle with a large eye. Size number 14 is very useful for chunkier yarns.

Complementary colour A colour which has the maximum contrast with another and found on opposite sides of the colour wheel (red is the complementary colour of green, blue of orange and yellow of violet).

Composite stitch A generic term for any stitch which relies on another for its base. A simple example is whipped running stitch where the foundation running stitch is worked first and the whipping in a separate section.

Crewel needle A sharp pointed needle with a long eye.

Dimensional paint A name for a variety of products which may be used to texture fabric surfaces. The patterns and textures formed by trailing or applying the paint become firm when dry. They are particularly useful where precise or delicate patterns are required. Available in a range of effects, from plain to glittery, the colours can be garish but may be mixed to subtle effect.

Discharge Removing colour from precoloured fabrics by chemical means. Household bleach or discharge pastes work well on cellulose fibres such as cotton. The prepared paste can have colour added so that the new colour can replace the ground fabric colour in the same process.

Disperse dyes An alternative name for transfer paints (see Transfer fabric paints)

Dressing A substance, sometimes starch or a type of gum, added to fabric in order to stiffen it and enhance its appearance. It should be thoroughly washed out of any material you intend colouring with fabric paint or dye.

Expanding medium (puff paint) There are various brand names for this substance which can be painted or printed onto a fabric surface. The expansion takes place when heat is applied in a number of ways such as with a hair dryer or a heat embossing tool which is particularly effective. Placing the fabric against an iron (on the reverse of the fabric) also works well. It is available in colours or in pots of neutral cream. Colour may be painted on afterwards using silk or permanent paints or acrylic.

Fabric paints These are usually water-based, non toxic paints for painting or printing on fabric. There is a vast range on the market suitable for many types of fabric. A huge colour choice, plus metallic, iridescent, and florescent ones, are available to tempt the embroiderer. Most paints are fixed by ironing.

Frames These are structures for stretching fabric tautly in order to keep the stitchery correctly tensioned or for ease of working for the embroiderer. A round tambour (ring) with an adjustable screw is suitable for hand and machine embroidery. Rectangular wooden or plastic frames vary enormously. Some trap or clamp the fabric tightly between two layers, while others allow the cloth to be pinned, stapled or laced around the edge.

Fastening on and off Methods used when commencing and finishing stitching. In most cases, begin stitching by fastening on at the back of the fabric by working tiny double stitches, or darning into the cloth or existing stitches. A knot at the end of the thread plus a double stitch is acceptable as long as it does not show through or cobble the right side of the fabric. To fasten off, take your thread through to the back and work a few small stitches as inconspicuously as possible.

Grid Superimposing a grid over an existing drawing allows you to enlarge a design. Scale-up the grid to the required size and re-draw the design accurately in the corresponding squares.

Gum arabic Sap from trees used as a binding medium for water-based paints. When applied to paper and mixed with other media, it cracks to produce textural effects.

Heat embossing tool A useful tool for concentrating heat in required areas. The small nozzle emits a fierce heat which can be used with greater precision and intensity than a hair drier for expanding mediums, plastics or 'Tyvek'. Beware of scorching.

Image A figurative, patterned or abstract visual concept, portrayed two-dimensionally.

Insertion stitches or faggoting Stitches used to make an open or decorative seam. The edges of fabric with narrow hems are placed opposite each other and tacked (leaving the required space between) onto a piece of parchment or paper. Stitches can be worked from one edge to the other without stitching into the paper, resulting in a lacy band joining the two fabrics.

Iridescent colour Colours which shimmer and change to display a spectrum of colour such as those of the rainbow. Iridescent powders can be mixed with gum arabic for painting on paper or 'Ormaline' or other mediums for applying on fabric. The colour can be fixed by ironing. Iridescent crayons and paints can be applied to cellophane before the ironing process for lustrous effects.

Machine lace A term referring to free machine embroidered patterns worked on soluble fabrics.

Masking fluid A fluid which can be painted onto paper to mask certain lines or areas of the design in order to resist watercolour paint which can be applied on top. It can be rubbed away using a finger or putty rubber.

Medium Any suitable material (such as oil, water, wax etc.) with which pigment is mixed to make it usable. In a more general sense it refers to the material from which a piece of work is created, for example acrylics or pastels.

Metallic foils Thin metallic layers supported by a heat resistant transparent film. The foil adheres to the surface by means of glue or fusible web which is applied to the surface and the foil placed on top, shiny side uppermost. Placing baking parchment over the foil is an extra precaution before ironing on a wool heat (no hotter). For subtle effects make light strokes with the iron. Foils are available from specialist craft suppliers but some computer heat foils can be used for non functional items.

Motif A distinctive feature of a design or unit of pattern.

Monochrome A painting or design created from one colour.

Ormoline A medium which can be mixed with iridescent and metallic powders for printing or painting on fabric.

Pattern A unit of design repeated in orderly or random groupings.

Pigments The colouring matter which is mixed with other substances to form media such as paints or pencils. Originally derived from natural sources, they are usually chemically based.

Polyester cotton A fabric woven in cotton and polyester (synthetic) yarns.

PVA glue or marvin medium (equivalent makes in the USA are Sobo Glue and Elmer's Glue). A non-toxic, very good, strong all-purpose glue which dries transparent and shiny. It can be diluted with water and mixed with colour to make textured surfaces.

Primary colours Colours which cannot be made by mixing together other colours i.e. red, blue and yellow.

Procion powder A dye powder normally used for dyeing fabrics when following the correct recipe containing a fixative. When mixed with cold water it produces marvellous colours for designing, but should be handled carefully with rubber gloves.

Resist A barrier, such as wax, masking tape or masking fluid, applied to a background, blocking colour from the covered areas.

Rouleau In this book a rouleau means a fabric strip cut on the bias which has been machined and turned to make a hollow tube. Used for ties and trims on fashion accessories, they can be padded with cord or partially covered with machine stitches.

Scrim Open weave fabric of cotton, linen or hessian which can be pulled to make holes. Available in a variety of thicknesses and textures from very delicate to coarse.

Shot fabrics These are fabrics where the warp is one colour and the weft another which results in a surface that changes in tone according to the play of light.

Slubbed A thread spun with irregular lumps or thick areas.

Soldering iron A heat tool which is most effective when used with fabrics such as synthetics which respond to heat. For safety and ease of working the fabrics may be placed in a frame and marks, holes or textured surfaces may be achieved by 'drawing' or 'bruising' with the soldering iron. There are also specialist craft 'pyrography' irons available which have interchangeable patterned ends which can 'brand' patterns into surfaces. Beware of toxic fumes, wear a mask and work in a well ventilated space.

Soluble fabric There are three forms of this fabric on the market, each are soluble in cold, hot and boiling water. The first is a thin plastic material which must be protected from accidental spillages. There is also a new film which comes in two thicknesses; the thin film dissolves in cold water and the thicker 'Aquafilm' super in hot. 'Solvron' is another slightly less substantial fabric, similar in feel to the boiling kind, which also disappears under very hot water. The boiling water fabric is an 'organdy' type of cloth which seems to withstand more layering of machine stitching (plus hand stitches) than the cold water-soluble fabric. This will, of course, only dissolve in boiling water.

Stiletto A sharp pointed tool used for making holes in fabric to ease thicker threads through or for making eyelet holes.

Stylised The adaptation of an image within the constraints of a particular style.

Symmetry A shape in which each half is a mirror image of the other and is balanced about a central axis.

Tacking or basting A long straight stitch.

Texture A quality of surface, such as rough, smooth or ridged, descriptive of the many complex fabrics in this book.

Texture gels Non toxic light modelling pastes which have a variety of textural additions to thicken and change the surface to be painted. The range includes those with iridescent, metallic, grainy and flaky qualities. They can be mixed with other coloured acrylics, powders and fabric paints.

Tissue A fine translucent paper. In the context of stitched images this means a fine shimmering fabric made from metallic or lurex threads.

Tone The degree of lightness or darkness of a colour.

Transfer fabric paints and crayons or disperse dyes These can be used to create patterns on a smooth paper and when dry, ironed onto a suitable fabric.

'Tyvek' A fibrous sheet designed for durability and strength in archival work, building protection and for strong mail envelopes. It shrinks and distorts with heat – methods include ironing between layers of baking parchment and applying heat with a hair dryer or heat embossing tool, producing spectacular effects.

Further Reading

Jan Beaney, *Art of the Needle*, Century, London 1988

Jan Beaney, *Stitches: New Approaches*, B.T. Batsford 1985

Jan Beaney, *Vanishing Act*, Double Trouble Enterprises 1997

Jane Dunnewold, *Complex Cloth: A Comprehensive Guide to Surface Design*, Fiber Studio Press 1996

John Gillow and Nicholas Barnard, *Traditional Indian Textiles*, Thames and Hudson 1991

Jean Ray Laury, *Imagery on Fabric*, C and T Publishing Inc. 1997

Jean Littlejohn, *Voluptuous Velvet*, Double Trouble Enterprises 1997

Sheila Paine, *Embroidered Textiles, Traditional Patterns from Five Continents*, Thames and Hudson 1990

Barbara Lee Smith, *Celebrating the Stitch: Contemporary Embroidery of North America*, The Taunton Press 1991

Barbara Snook, *Embroidery Stitches*, B.T. Batsford 1992

Mary Thomas, *Mary Thomas's Dictionary of Embroidery Stitches*, Hodder and Stoughton 1993

Art Textiles of the World, (ed. Matthew Kounis), Telos Art Publications 1996

100 Embroidery Stitches, J & P Coats Ltd., Revised Edition 1981

5,000 Years of Textiles, (ed. Jennifer Harris) British Museum Press 1993

List of Suppliers

The authors use a wide range of silk and wollen yarns from Texere threads and in the main these have been coloured by the 'all in one' easy-to-use thirty minute dye process from Omega Dyes. They have also used threads supplied by the following:

Threads

Barnyarns
Canal Wharf
Bondgate Green
North Yorkshire
HG4 1AQ
Tel: 0870 870 8586
(general embroidery supplies)

Coats Crafts UK
PO Box 22
Lingfield House
McMullen Road
Darlington
Co Durham DL1 1YQ
Tel: 01325 394 287
(hand embroidery, crochet and machine threads, including Kreinik yarns, information and stockists)

De Haviland Embroidery
27 Old Gloucester Street
London WC1 3XX

Margaret Beal Embroidery
28 Leigh Road
Andover
Hants SP10 2AP
Tel: 01246 365102
(heated stencil cutters)

Mace and Nairn
PO Box 5626
Northampton NN7 2BF
Tel: 01604 864869
(general embroidery supplies)

Mulberry Silks
Patricia Wood
Silkwood
4 Park Close
Tetbury
Gloucestershire GL8 8HS
Tel: 01666 503438

The Silk Route
Cross Cottage (E)
Cross Lane
Frimley Green
Surrey GU16 6LN
Tel: 01252 835781

Stef Francis
Waverley
High Rocombe
Stokeinteignhead
Newton Abbot
Devon TQ12 4QL
Tel: 01803 323004

Texere Threads
College Mills
Barkerend Road
Bradford BD3 9AQ
Tel: 01274 722191

Oliver Twists
22 Phoenix Road
Crowther
Washington
Tyne & Wear NE38 0AD
Tel: 0191 4166016
(shaded threads)

Variegations
Rose Cottage
Harper Royd Lane
Norland
Halifax HX6 3QQ
Tel: 01422 832411
(full range of threads)

Fabrics and general embroidery supplies

Bombay Stores
Bombay Buildings
Shearbridge Road
Bradford
West Yorkshire BD7 1NX
Tel: 01274 729993
(fabrics and threads)

Borovicks Fabrics Limited
16 Berwick Street
London W1V 4HP
Tel: 020 7437 2180

Gillsew
Boundary House
Moor Common
Lane End
High Wycombe
Buckinghamshire HP14 3HR
Tel: 01494 881886
(general supplies including fabric paints)

Husqvarna Studio
90 Lower Parliament Street
Nottingham NG1 1EH
Tel: 0115 9881550
('solusheet' soluble fabric)

Inca Studio Limited
10 Duke Street
Princes Risborough
Buckinghamshire HP27 0AT
Tel: 01844 343343
(general embroidery supplies)

John Lewis Partnership
278–306 Oxford Street
London W1A 1EX
Tel: 020 7629 7711

Rainbow Silks
6 Wheelers Yard
High Street
Great Missenden
Buckinghamshire HP16 0AL
Tel: 01494 862111

Strata
Copthorne
The Undercliffe
Sandgate
Kent CT20 3AT
Tel: 01303 245682
(Xpandaprint and Tyvek film, fabric, soft sculpt and chiffon scarves)

Winifred Cottage
17 Elms Road
Fleet
Hampshire GU51 3EG
Tel: 01252 617667
(threads, chiffon scarves, beads and dyes)

Supermend Limited
PO Box 300
Basildon
Essex SS4 3RT
Tel: 01268 271244
(bonding powder)

Whaleys (Bradford) Limited
Harris Court
Great Horton
Bradford
West Yorkshire BD7 4EQ
Tel: 01274 576718
(fabrics, including cold- and boiling-water soluble)

Paints, dyes and other materials

Art Van Go
1 Stevenage Road
Knebworth
Hertfordshire SG3 6AN
Tel: 01438 814946
(art supplies and metallic powders, ormaline, discharge paste, heat tools)

L Cornellison and Son Limited
105 Great Russell Street
London WC1B 3RY
Tel: 020 7636 1045
(general art supplies, metallic and iridescent powders, iridescent crayons and gouache)

Tonertex Foils
PO Box 3746
London N2 9DE
Tel: 020 8444 1992

Lowery Workstands
Bentley Lane
Grasby
Barnetby
North Lincolnshire DN38 6AW
Tel: 01652 628240
(paper string)

Omega Dyes
Myrtle Cottage
Powerstock
Bridport
Dorset DT6 3TD
Tel: 01308 485242

General information about new products and mail order suppliers can be found in *Embroidery* and *Stitch* magazines, both published by:
The Embroiderers' Guild
Apartment 41
Hampton Court Palace
East Molesey
Surrey KT8 9AU

See also *The Textile Directory*, which can be obtained from:
107 High Street
Evesham WR11 4EB
Tel: 01386 760406

Index